CODE, COMMUNITY, MINISTRY

SELECTED STUDIES FOR THE
PARISH MINISTER INTRODUCING
THE CODE OF CANON LAW

SECOND REVISED
EDITION

EDITED BY EDWARD G. PFNAUSCH

Canon Law Society of America
The Catholic University of America
Washington, D.C. 20064

CONTENTS

The Church's Sacramental Life

Sanctions in the Church

INTRODUCTION

A growing discovery in the post-Vatican II Church has been the pastoral potential to be found in the Church's law. Church law is broader than a set of canons or detailed prescriptions. It reflects the fundamental communion of the Church and is directed toward fostering the mission of all the people of God.

The promulgation of the revised Code of Canon Law for the Latin Church on January 25, 1983, and the Code of Canons of the Eastern Churches on October 18, 1990 by Pope John Paul II mark important steps on the road to discovering the potential of the law. In both documents of promulgation, *Sacrae disciplinae leges* and *Sacri Canones*, Pope John Paul II clearly states that these codes be important elements in implementing the spirit and teachings of the Second Vatican Council. These codes are meant to be instruments to promote the communion of all the Catholic Churches.

Law texts tend to be technical and dry. It takes an added effort at times to appreciate their pastoral significance, or to explore the opportunities that these two codes present to the Church for continuing the work of renewal based on the teachings of Vatican II. To help in this effort, a series of short studies have been put together. Many originated from the workshops conducted by the Canon Law Society of America in the summer of 1982 for diocesan administrators prior to the implementation of the 1983 Code. Others have been culled from various CLSA publications, including *Code of Canon Law: A Text and Commentary*, CLSA *Proceedings, Roman Replies and CLSA Advisory Opinions*. These short studies address the pastoral implications and opportunities of the 1983 Code, attempt to explain the 1983 Code's significance for various aspects of pastoral ministry, and sketch in broad strokes the numerous ecclesiastical structures which pastoral ministers often encounter.

The Canon Law Society of America is pleased to make these studies available to a wider audience. This second edition has been expanded and refined. With the promulgation of the Code of Canons of the Eastern Churches, it is the hope of the CLSA that similar studies will be forth coming to enlighten and assist both Eastern and Latin Catholics in realizing the pastoral potential of this new law. To that end the CLSA has completed a Latin-English edition of the Eastern Code.

A special word of appreciation is expressed to Bertram F. Griffin, J.C.D., Archdiocese of Portland-in-Oregon, who contributed many of these studies. Appreciation also is expressed to the other CLSA members who contributed studies or whose work is reprinted here from various CLSA copyrighted publications: Adam J. Maida, J.C.L., J.D., Archdiocese of Detroit; John A. Alesandro, J.C.D., Diocese of Rockville Centre; James H. Provost, J.C.D., The

Catholic University of America, Washington, D.C.; Kenneth E. Lasch, J.C.D., Diocese of Paterson; Thomas J. Green, J.C.D., The Catholic University of America, Washington, D.C.; Richard C. Cunningham, J.C.D., Archdiocese of Boston; Edward G. Pfnausch, J.C.D. Cand., The Catholic University of America, Washington, D.C.; John A. Renken, J.C.D., Diocese of Springfield, Illinois; John M. Huels, O.S.M., J.C.D., Chicago, Illinois; Joseph A. Janicki, J.C.D., Archdiocese of Milwaukee; Joseph A. Galante, J.C.D., Rome, Italy.

CANON LAW AND PASTORAL EXPERIENCE[1]

It is a maxim of the civil law, normally quoted by the unsuccessful party, that someone has stolen justice and hidden it in the law. How many of the Christian faithful expect a similar result when they encounter the canon law, namely that someone has stolen the Church and hidden it in the law? Given the juridical structure and literal application of the 1917 Code, such an expectation may have had a reasonable foundation in the experience of the faithful. But with the promulgation of the revised code, the insights of the Vatican Council that have been integrated in the code, and the training of canonists and theologians that has kept pace with these developments, the Christian faithful can rightfully expect a much more positive experience of canon law in the life of the Church. That will necessitate greater reflection, scholarship and integration among the Christian faithful than has heretofore been the case. Of necessity, it will include attention to the disciplines of organizational theory and the dynamics of communication and conflict resolution, which are not always visible elements of the canonical process.

Whatever one may decide are the disciplines that need to be integrated in making the experience of law in the Church uniquely pastoral, I am certain that this pastoral experience can only be achieved in the Church's life if there is a common commitment to this end. A pastoral experience of the law will not occur automatically and its occurrence must not be left to accident or be made dependent only on the good intent of the law maker, the interpreter, or the administrator. Perhaps it will really entail a genuine *metanoia* of each of us, law giver, interpreter, scholar, teacher, theologian, and recipient. *Metanoia* is not an automatic or accidental process. That the process must be conscious, is perhaps the underlying truth of John Courtney Murray's statement that the modern crisis in the Church is not one of authority nor of law but one of community.

The question for our future is how do we create a broad based, credible experience of our law as pastoral? It will not be enough to simply say that the canonical system is pastoral because it is inextricably bound to a theology and an ecclesiology, which it serves (cf. *Comm.* 2 [1970]: 23-28). Nor is it enough to promulgate the code as, not an end in itself, but an instrument to preserve individual and social order in the Church, such order serving and maintaining the primacy of the supernatural reality of the Church and the primacy of love, grace and charism (cf. apos. const., John Paul II, *Sacrae disciplinae leges*, 25

---

[1]From: *Reflections: On the Occasion of the 50th Anniversary*, Richard G. Cunningham, ed. (Washington, D.C.: Canon Law Society of America, 1988) 39-42.

January 1983). Nor will analytical scholarship and theological commentary be enough. I think that scholars, pastors, and members of the Church will need to discover both cognitively and experientially how we create pastoral canonical experiences.

These observations and expectations are born of my hopes and experiences. I offer these thoughts for your reflection as representative of a canonist's and a pastor's struggle to be Church, to participate in Church, to create a community which calls itself Church, even, or especially, in times of conflict.

Whether canonical encounters are experienced as pastoral depends on the consciously integrated sacramental and ecclesial self-awareness of the parties more than it does on the norms of the law. While all of us, through baptism, receive the grace to realize a sacramental reality in life, I suspect that few of us, regardless of title or function, have consistent, mature, theologically integrated lives. Therefore, in creating an experience of our law as pastoral, our major hope must lie in greater effort toward reflective action on our part when we encounter the law in our lives, or when the law seeks to intrude itself on our lives.

I am reminded of an axiom from my law school days. One of the first cliches we learned from our professors was, "Who frames the issue, wins the case." The second axiom we learned was that legal issues were to be resolved by applying the law to the facts. "Law plus the facts" allowed us to identify and solve legal issues. I sometimes wonder if these rules of our American legal system have not carried over into the way we Americans approach canonical issues so as to deprive us of the pastoral experience of law which promotes and protects the rights and values of the community. As I reflect on this, I wonder if we might not be doing the exact opposite of Pope John Paul II's stated purposes of the law in his promulgation constitution, *Sacrae disciplinae leges*, namely elevating the law to an end in itself as opposed to using it only in service of community and in the creation of community.

Would our experience of the law be more creative of community, more *communio*, if we perceived law as truly flowing out of experience and theology rather than a narrow legalism where law is applied to life (facts) simply to maintain order? If we "frame the issue" differently does the *communio* win, perhaps to the detriment of the parties, but to the benefit of the whole, of us all? And should this not be the preferred methodology of a law in service to community, namely to begin with the facts, as every lawyer must, but then to factor in the values creative of, and supportive of, community in order to determine what the relevant law in a given case should or ought to be?

Such a perspective provides a good beginning but, perhaps it is not enough. There must be a perceivable difference in the person as well as the methodology, if the canonical experience is to be unique. Ultimately, the sacramental self-awareness, perceptions, and expectations of the law maker, the interpreter, and the recipient of the law create the experience. While each according to status may have a different role in a canonical context, each because of baptism and the responsibilities of membership in the *communio*, must create a consistent and appropriately ecclesial approach to and expectation of canon law and process. Our community experience will not be uniquely pastoral unless there exists within each and among each a shared vision mutually enriched by the other's experience and discovered not in the arbitrary exercise of authority, power, contentiousness, independence, or defiance, but in the humility and simplicity characteristic of the pilgrim Church whose authority is divine, held in sacramental bond, and not overly based on person or on title.

The creation of this shared vision is a heavy challenge to our catechesis and canonical training. Mere study of the code alone will not provide it. But life without the code does not provide it either. Rather, the catechesis and the training must each strive to reflect true life, the common experience of the faithful trying to create *communio*. The two must become one, so that our law is perceived as pastoral and, in fact, is pastoral, but pastoral by being rooted in the common experience of each of us, be we legislator, interpreter, administrator, scholar, teacher, or subject of the law.

Our individual expectations or experience of canon law is birthed by our ecclesial world view. This, of course, assumes that our ecclesial world view enables us to differentiate our expectations of canonical experiences from those of our common law, and from political, cultural, or other professional experience. This is where problems creep in, because we, as Americans, have only one other legal system with which to compare our canonical system. And if we attempt to understand the latter by comparison to the former, not only does the analogy pale, if fails. For example, consider how the following issues in our canon law could be approached:

When a lay person approaches a marriage tribunal, does she or he expect to explore the existence or non-existence of a sacrament, or does he or she simply want the public approval of the Church and the freedom to remarry within the Church, with a Church ceremony?

Within the tribunal, do canon lawyers create forms and procedures that focus on numerical evaluation and standardization in such a way that persons become the instrumentality of tribunal practice? Is more energy spent on assumptions of appellate reviewers related to numbers of annulments than on the struggle of placing contemporary meaning in facts and theology and ecclesial ideals?

When time comes to divest of a major apostolate or piece of property, is the canonical administrator's approach "what formalities must I go through to get Rome to rubber-stamp this?" Or is it, what effect will this transaction (fact) have on the institutional mission of the Church in this institutionally based society (theology and fact)?

When such issues arise, a pastor needs to have a self perception of the sacramental role of servanthood and as expeditor and promoter of *communio* even in conflict. This is a different role than his role as executive or administrator, although the two are related. Coupled with this perception, he must also have the skill to manage canonical encounters and even personal strife consistently with this end.

If, in these tribunal examples, judge, advocate, and the parties were catechized to fact plus sacramental experience to achieve law and we reflected on whether our processes promote the pastoral creation of *communio* as distinct from what is permissible according to a norm, would we credibly experience the *salus animarum* of the law? Or, to take the alienation example, does more *communio* result if the administrator first focuses on the effect such a transaction will have on the apostolic future of the juridic person and its ability to play a part in society, both civil and ecclesial? And only after such issues are dealt with, does the administrator move on to consider what is the legal norm in this regard.

The pastor must recognize that the subtle but powerful drive for hierarchical order may be in conflict with the creation of *communio*. He must distinguish creative conflict from destructive conflict. He, too, is vulnerable, perhaps more than others, to use the law as the mere creator of order, rather than as ecclesially exhortative, and fully pastoral. Finally, protection of the *communio* should also avoid the deductive mechanical reading of all norms as if they were statutes. There is that which the law requires and that which the law allows; the pastor must see the difference between the two.

The problem is not limited to the clergy or religious. As indicated in the tribunal examples that I gave above, the lay person must also be able to differentiate expectations of canonical process from participatory democracy and the common law adversarial processes.

In addition to the capacity of individuals to differentiate ecclesial norms and expectations, it is necessary to have a mutually shared ecclesial vision and expectation of law and canonical processes. While cultural expectations are inextricable, they may not be more controlling than ecclesial ones. Perhaps the keystone of the mutually shared vision is the understanding that canon law is essentially a law for the *communio* and does not focus on the individual as such. The ultimate right is vested in the *communio*, with each of us, according to baptism and status, sharing certain dimensions of the right. In the paradigm, an adversarial juxtaposition of rights is inappropriate.

This is not so in our common law legal system. For example, in common law, rights (those of the state and of the individual) are based on social contract, political power, delegation, or non-delegation. In our common law system, rights are adversarial and sometimes mutually exclusive. The civil legal process creates winners and losers through a balancing process. If, in a canonical context, individual rights were pitted one against the other, whether it is pastor against individual or diocese, or one practice pitted against another, forcing a "balancing of rights" to determine a winner or a loser, violence is done to the *communio* as well as to the purpose of the Church's law. While in most canonical contests, there is an apparent conflict of rights, all concerned need to guard against an unexamined acceptance of this as the enduring and controlling characterization of the situation.

While we share a common ecclesial vision, we must equally share a mutual understanding of the pluralism of our roles. For example, a Catholic university is not the same as a Catholic elementary or secondary school. The code recognizes this by treating them differently. Different standards as to catechesis must be applied to them. A hospital's Catholicity is not expressed, implemented, or determined in the same way a parish's identity would be. What makes a parish community "Catholic" is not necessarily what makes a hospital "Catholic" and care must be taken to treat them differently as well.

The point of these musings is to suggest a basic question: When Church law is practiced, who is the client? An individual or group of individuals, or the Church? How do I sacramentally perceive the situation? How is it approached?

If the approach, *ab initio*, is "what does the code say?" one creates the possibility that a large analysis will be forced onto a situation, depriving it of its pastoral uniqueness. If one puts energy into what is the underlying ecclesial reality and secondarily seeks norms, then a religious experience creative of *communio* may be more possible.

The significant question when one approaches the analysis of any problem is: What values are to be protected? This is distinctly different from asking what rights need to be balanced or advanced. The next question, then, is: Are those values based on a shared ecclesiology or theology or are they personal agendas? It seems to me that, in the Church and its legal system, one solves problems by analyzing what ecclesial values are at risk as opposed to weighing rights, one against the other. Not only is the process different, but the result will be different from that of other legal systems that focus primarily on justice whereas our ecclesial legal system seeks the unity and order of *communio*. For me, the challenge of the next era is to create experientially that uniqueness, to find the promise of the Church once again in its law.

MOST REV. ADAM J. MAIDA, J.C.L.
Detroit, Michigan

RENEWAL AND REFORM[1]

The law is not meant to be a text for academic rumination but an effective instrument to guide the life of the people of God. The code is so deeply rooted in the decrees of Vatican II that it's practical intent should be obvious—the promotion of pastoral renewal and reform.

The Church's first authoritative codification was promulgated seventeen years after the turn of the century. It implemented the current view of the Church and its mission, particularly in the light of Vatican Council I and development during the ensuing decades. The Church's second authoritative codification has been promulgated seventeen years before the same century draws to a close. It too hopes to implement a contemporary understanding of the Church and its mission, expressed so carefully in Vatican Council II and subsequent teaching. As law has done from the beginning, the code tries to articulate the order and discipline that the Church needs at this time in salvation history. The message of the code is clear: the Church needs continued renewal and reform. How can a code of law hope to assist the Church to achieve such a noble goal?

Like other periods of church reform, the post-Vatican II Church requires laws to stabilize long-term shifts of practice and discipline. The code seeks to achieve this goal by clarifying rights and duties. Clarity is needed in order to dispel the confusion that has arisen prior to and after the council. It was difficult even for trained pastoral ministers to keep track of the Church's regulations during the quarter-century preceding the promulgation. The code collects into a single volume all of the juridic changes that have occurred as part of the Church's effort at self-renewal. In doing so, it integrates them into the overall canonical tradition. The laws, so clarified, are not so vague and perplexing as before.

The code does not reproduce all of the Church's legal history. It distills past decrees into a fairly simple system. Many pastoral ministers may have to admit that they have not even read all of the conciliar decrees much less studied, synthesized, and appropriated them. At least in regard to matters of juridic import, the code provides a synthesis that should spark more intensive study of as well as fidelity to the foundations of the conciliar reform. This synthesis is not buried in a textual labyrinth. It is available in the vernacular not only to pastoral ministers but to all the people of God. One of the simplest means of promoting rights in the Church is to give to those endowed

[1]From: *The Code of Canon Law: A Text and Commentary*, James A. Coriden, et al., ed. (Mahwah, N.J.: Paulist Press, 1985) 20-22.

with such rights a book which articulates them.

Principles or norms that are clear, fairly simple, and readily available for consultation and guidance are the classic requirements of any institutional reform. The code contributes a great deal to the fulfillment of these needs. It is a contribution that is necessarily temporary. History is not likely to alter its inexorable course. Church practice will continue to evolve and, with it, canon law. The code will require ongoing interpretation, amendment and, eventually, abrogation. Its clarity will be dulled, its simplicity marred, and the resultant complexity will make it more difficult for those who are not canonists to be knowledgeable about extant law. Nonetheless, for the moment, the revised code will accomplish its important task and spur on the process of renewal.

Principally, the revised law serves to strengthen and solidify present-day ecclesial structures and trends. When certain innovations are stabilized, they cease to be thought of as experimental and begin to have a long-term effect. This steadying function provides a new stimulus to make the structures work, highlights the important values involved, deepens the motivation of the participants, and provides accountability systems for the long haul. The following are a few examples of the beneficial developments to be found in the revised code:

a. the reliance on the image of the Church as the people of God, whose members are sacramentally commissioned to carry out the threefold mission of Christ as priest, prophet, and king;

b. the recognition of the fundamental equality of individual Christians and the rights and responsibilities that flow from baptism and confirmation;

c. the enhanced role of lay persons in the Church;

d. the shift from an emphasis on persons endowed with authority to juridically recognized functions of service;

e. the promotion of the value of subsidiarity in the hierarchical communion and an acceptance of the resultant structural pluralism;

f. the stress on the particular church as a "portion of the people of God" (*portio populi Dei*) and the importance of the diocesan bishop and particular law;

g. the implementation of structures of consultation at all levels of the Church;

h. the promotion of accountability in regard to temporalities;

i. the priority given to pastoral care and the introduction of greater flexibility into canonical institutes in order to facilitate the realization of the Church's fundamental mission (e.g., in parish structures, parish personnel, the celebration of the sacraments, the revision of ecclesiastical penalties).

7

Some may find this role of law hard to accept. For them law is cold and unyielding, impersonal and static, ultimately devoid of love and the Spirit. It cannot achieve reform; if anything, it thwarts reform, impedes growth, and retards progress. This raises an attitudinal (and ultimately theological) problem whose impact on the success of the revised code is crucial. Even with its inevitable gaps and flaws, the code is a sound pastoral document that can achieve its purpose. Whether it does, however, depends on its reception by the people of God, particularly by pastoral ministers. Receptivity to the code depends on the individual's attitude toward the role of law in the Church. The question of attitude is a very profound issue with a pervasive impact on the whole canonical system.

There are many attitudes in the contemporary Church that may distort the law and nullify its ecclesial effect. There are those who are ignorant of, or consciously dismiss, history. They are like little children playing with shells on the beach, unaware that behind them stretches the vast sea of knowledge that has cast their playthings before them. There are those who fail to grasp the theological underpinnings of church law. Their uninformed application of the law identifies them as the voluntarists of our present day, all too ready to exercise power but bored by the tedium of understanding. There are neo-juridicists who have welcomed the promulgation of the code as if it would restore some long-forgotten, idyllic, and, in the end, imaginary time of uniformity and regimentation. They do not appreciate the implications of the legal system found in the code. Finally, there are antinomians, so foolishly imprisoned by the very culture they hope to evangelize. They reject all that is "institutional" as alien to the gospel, blithely unconcerned that they are part of the historical pendulum of reaction against authority and perplexed by the need to live out the faith in a "visible" Church.

If these attitudes predominate, the code will not achieve its true purpose of strengthening conciliar aims, solidifying desirable ecclesial structures, and promoting the rights and responsibilities of all in the Church. A new attitude toward law is needed, Paul VI's "new way of thinking." This element of the revision process cannot be achieved by the Pontifical Commission for the Interpretation of Legal Texts, by consultation, or by theological or canonical experts. It can be achieved only by persons of faith who receive the law, assimilate it, apply it, and obey it.

The code does not masquerade as the means of salvation. Salvation remains always and only the gift of God. Nonetheless, the law does represent for the people of God part of the contemporary way of "putting on Christ"; the Church's vision of itself at this moment in its history. It defines and regulates the structures of church order and discipline, its decisions about itself, and its organization. Canon law is a symbol of the Church's unwillingness to abandon the weighty implications of Christ's incarnation or to relegate

8

God's action to the purely spiritual realm. For those who accept the code into their lives in an authentic manner, it provides an identifiable ground of commonality with the other members of the Church, underlines the basis of their identity as the people of God, and articulates legitimate expectations. In other words, the code does not itself continue the conciliar reform—it simply offers an opportunity and a means to achieve that end. How well the opportunity is utilized depends on the people of the Church in this task, the cherished goal of its authors will be happily achieved.

When the elders in Jerusalem acceded to many of the norms proposed by St. Paul for his Gentile converts, they felt that they had made a good determination, a practical decision that was faithful to Jesus and, therefore, imbued with the Holy Spirit. This decision was communicated to the Christians at Antioch, accepted by them, and faithfully implemented. Later on, when the long-term effect of the norms had been achieved and the Church had expanded throughout the Mediterranean, the original rules were hardly alluded to; some in fact were abandoned in favor of newer regulations. While law remains, individual laws have a life that is ephemeral at best. The promulgation of the 1983 Code is really not so different from that ancient letter to the Antiochians. Those who come to understand the canons and implement them properly might very well join with the elders of the Jerusalem community in saying: "Today, this way of putting on Christ, this way of being Church, seems good to us and to the Holy Spirit."

JOHN A. ALESANDRO, J.C.D.
Rockville Centre, New York

APPROACHING THE REVISED CODE

Approaching the revised code can be compared to approaching a new wine. We know it comes from historic soil, tested vines, and an estate with experience in producing this kind of thing. Yet still we approach it carefully, first sipping to get the initial taste; then savoring a second sip to discover the nuance. Finally, we must decide how to store and, eventually, consume the product.

So it is with the recently promulgated revised code. Its roots extend back through Christian tradition to the Scriptures themselves. It comes from centuries of legal tradition within the Catholic community. The revised code itself is the product of a complicated process conducted on behalf of the Holy See and reaching out for consultation with bishops and experts from around the world. But what is the final product like? Let me share a first sip with you, and then a more nuanced taste. Finally, let me suggest some possibilities for receiving the revised code in this country.

AN OVERVIEW

Influence of Vatican II

When John XXIII called for an "aggiornamento" of the Code of Canon Law, he saw it as a way of implementing in the practical life of the Church the renewal he was inaugurating in the Catholic Church. In many ways the revised code is remarkably faithful to the decisions of Second Vatican Council, the touchstone of John's renewal.

The revised law provides a common status for all in the Church, based on their baptism and directed toward their involvement in the mission of the Church. The distinctions of clergy and laity remain, but are placed in a new context. Instead of building the whole legal structure on the differences between clergy and laity as the 1917 Code did, this revised law begins with the common dignity of all the baptized and puts distinctions in terms of service and ministry. Responsibilities and rights of all Christians are spelled out in what for canon law is a new experience of a kind of "bill of rights". Theoretically, involvement in Church work is open to any Christian provided the person has the necessary qualifications. The special responsibilities that arise from one's state in life, for example, parenthood, are given explicit recognition.

The role of lay persons receives increased attention in the code, as it did in Vatican II. Their responsibility for spreading the Gospel in every walk of life is recalled. Their rights to the spiritual goods of the Church, especially the Word of the God and the sacraments, form the basis for several innovations in how ministry is to be structured, and even the variety of persons who may perform official Church ministry.

One of the major issues at Vatican II was the relationship of the diocesan bishops with Rome. The collegiality of bishops and the role of the diocesan bishop within his local church were major advances of the council. These are reflected in many striking ways in the revised code. The local bishop has considerable freedom of action. Many restrictions on his initiative and discretion have been removed and he is encourage to apply the law to the local conditions of his church, always working within the framework of the code and directives from the Vatican.

As he does this, the bishop is called to a renewed sense of Church as a community of persons rather than his own fiefdom or possession. Applying the people-centered definition of a diocese which comes from Vatican II, the revised code extends this approach to its definition of a parish. No longer just an administrative division of the diocese, as it could be considered under the old code, the parish is now presented as a community of persons with their own life and mission. The assignment of clergy, development of programs, and determination of membership in parish communities is more flexible under the revised law, but is to fit within the general framework of this communitarian approach. If there are not enough priests to have a resident pastor in each parish, for example, the parish need not be closed; a person who is not a priest, whether a deacon, a religious or lay woman or man, can be given the daily pastoral care within that community.

Compromise

If the revised code is faithful to Vatican II, it is also faithful to one of the key experiences of the council as well: compromise. The document is clearly a compromise on many issues debated at the council, or debated even before then among canon lawyers. For example, at Vatican II the role of episcopal conferences was hotly debated. Some saw it as a weakening of the role of the local bishop; others, as a threat to the role of the Holy See. Still, episcopal conferences were set up and have proven to be a major benefit to the life of the Church in many areas of the world.

The revised code keeps the episcopal conference structure, and calls on conferences to set policy in a variety of issues. But the revision process reflected the same tensions over the role of the conferences and the law shows the results of this compromise. The conference can bind local dioceses in only a few matters. On the other hand, they are free to develop a spirit of mutual understanding and cooperation, and can continue to develop as major influences in the life of the Church. What is in the law does not exhaust the possibilities of what can become effective through creative action.

Marriage tribunal procedures are another example of compromise. Many

11

of the advances contained in the American Procedural Norms have now been extended to the Church universal. On the other hand, the requirement that every case be reviewed by a panel of three judges has been reimposed on the church courts in this country. Dioceses across the nation are now exploring ways to live with this compromise.

A third area of compromise concerns church finances. The revised code does not address the Vatican's finances. Presumably, those are governed by special norms for the Roman Curia and the Vatican City State. The code's laws do affect local dioceses, however, and show the influence of a debate over the most appropriate way to fund diocesan operations. The Code Commission's secretariat argued that the canonical tradition puts first emphasis on free-will offerings of the faithful. Many American dioceses do rely heavily on this, whether through an annual fund drive or by more sophisticated long-term giving programs of annuities and wills. But a number of the Code Commission members, primarily diocesan bishops themselves, wanted to regularize a practice which is also common in this country whereby dioceses tax a percentage of parish income. This, under the revised code, will finally become legal in church law.

Problem Areas

If the code is marked by compromises, it is also plagued with some issues which may become problems for the Church in the United States. The most publicly noted one is the question of "mandate" for teachers of theology in colleges and universities. The European mentality, rooted in close Church-state relations where the government pays the teachers but the Church retains control over who is named to teach, has predominated in the approach to Catholic higher education even though a majority to the world's Catholic institutions of learning are in this country. Ways of working with this new law are being explored with civil law experts.

Another problem area is the role of consultative bodies such a priests' councils, diocesan pastoral councils, and parish councils. The revised code can be read as giving the bishop (or pastor, at the parish level) a much more controlling role in these bodies than is congenial to the American experience. The struggles of the years since the council to implement what many rightly understood as shared responsibility and a greater role for priests and lay persons in the life of the Church could be lost if the revised code is not interpreted very carefully.

A third problem could be hiding in the law on the sale of church property. While it does not change radically the previous practice, it does clarify some aspects of the law which were mercifully vague heretofore, and might cause religious communities and various church institutions some additional headaches in today's business climate.

Beneath these more immediate aspects of the revised code there are some challenging nuances which deserve to be addressed. Like savoring a wine, there are bitter and sweet impressions when studying this document.

Law for Disciples

It is, underneath all its traditional language and legal formulation, an attempt to develop a law for disciples. A lot of the restrictive details of the former code have been done away with. The role of penalties or sanctions in church law has been dramatically reduced. Although procedures for accountability do exist, teeth to enforce them are lacking or relatively weak. Local adaptation is stressed, although with caution.

What this means is that if the revised code is going to work, it will be because it is accepted by a faith community which sees in it an instrument to promote its following of the Lord. Rather than a set of laws for a government to enforce, this code is intended as a discipline for a people who are themselves committed to discipleship.

If a church official is not a person of faith, this law could be circumvented, obstructed, or ignored. For a community more interested in power politics than proclaiming the Word, the law can be a source of frustration or even alienation. This is a risk the revisers of the code decided to take, for it is the risk the council (and Christ!) have invited us to undertake. Disciples are called to faith, not lording it over others.

New Way of Thinking

Perhaps this illustrates a second nuance in the revised code. It is an attempt to reflect a new way of thinking, that "new habit of mind" which Paul VI charged the Code Commission to implement when he set them upon their task at the conclusion of Vatican II. A new way of thinking takes time to absorb, for when we deal with law we deal with a very conservative aspect of life and often we miss the nuance this new way of thinking requires.

A first expression of this new thinking is in the whole understanding of the Church which is reflected in the code. The 1917 Code clearly addressed the Church as a monarchy, a religious government with institutions stretching from the universal to the most local neighborhood levels. The revised code attempts to take seriously the sense of Church as a communion, a bonding together of people in the Lord and with one another at various levels of their Church experience. Many of the structures of the old code are still there, but the attempt has been made to address them in a new context.

Another expression of the new way of thinking is in the approach to ministry. Church office is no longer restricted just to clergy. The rights of the faithful to the Word and sacraments can lead to lay people staffing parishes, parents exercising greater responsibility in preparing their children for Christian life, and the whole community getting involved in marriage preparation. Empowerment of the Church to carry out the three-fold work of Christ, teaching, sanctifying and transforming the world to his rule, is as central to this code as the restrictive controls were to the 1917 version.

A third impact of the new way of thinking is how the revised law deals with other Christians. In the 1917 law, they were considered "bad Catholics", bound by the restrictions of the Catholic Church's law but not able to benefit from rights within the Church. The revised code is more realistic. Other Christians are other Christians, not bad Catholics. They are not bound by the restrictions in Catholic Church law, but are able to benefit from a number of rights within the Church if they so desire—for example, the right to hear the Word preached, or to receive certain sacraments under conditions which respect ecumenical sensitivities and our own tradition.

Challenge and Opportunity

As a law of disciples and a new way of thinking, the revised code is an important opportunity for the Church everywhere, including in this country. What we do with that opportunity, however, may well determine whether we have caught these nuances. The revision process at the Vatican illustrates how difficult it can be to think anew as disciples.

The code has been revised in a rather unique system, covered by secrecy which is designed to leak, consulting bishops around the world but influenced by politics with civil governments and political pressures within the Church structure. It was ostensibly the work of a commission, but a commission whose members were often too occupied elsewhere to spend quality time working on the product, and many of whose members are removed from pastoral life. The final product was reexamined by the pope and a select group of advisors who remained anonymous, a process subject to much intrigue and pressure. The idea of consultation was good, but the practice illustrates how hard it is to adopt a new way of thinking while immersed in system which served the old as well.

What about ourselves? Will the opportunity to implement Vatican II's renewal in the very legal structures of the Church bring forth a new way of doing this, recognizing the common dignity and responsibility of all disciples? Or, will we slip into the old way of doing things, leaving it up to the "experts", the bishops and their staffs or the episcopal conference, to determine how the implementation is to be done? There are a number of practical decisions to be made, adaptations of the law to be worked out, and structures to be evaluated and revised.

The revised code continues the ancient Christian tradition of making laws in synods and councils. But it also provides for administrative decrees which bishops can issue on their own, with or without consulting anyone. Only in a very few cases must the bishop consult with specified groups before issuing a decision. The opportunity in this new way of thinking is for bishops and the bishops' conference to take advantage of the possibilities as we have never been able to do it before, and to make the implementation of the revised code an experience of discipleship.

IMPLEMENTING THE CODE

New wine should not be put into old wine skins. It takes a new skin, if it is not to burst the old and be lost. Something similar applies to the revised code. The new way of thinking, the opportunity for discipleship, takes more than the old way of doing things if it will survive and meet the expectations that marked John XXIII's call for the revised code.

There has been a kind of anti-nominanism since the council, an attitude that law had no place in Church life. People have been alienated by outmoded procedures, or experiences in which their expectations for new life were dashed by an authority's appeal to old legalisms. The attitude toward the revised code has often been one of "ho-hum", or a bemused look at stewards rearranging deck chairs on the Titanic.

Recently, I have discovered new interest in church law. A group of theology students reported at the end of last semester they were amazed at how pastoral and creative the revised code can be. During a series of workshops on the revised code for diocesan administrators, the experience was repeated over and over of people awakening to the fact that this is not a law of "musts", but really is a new way of thinking. It does hold promise for promoting the pastoral life of the Church and setting the stage for more dynamic mission by the Catholic community.

The difference lies in our attitude. Disciples are not timid; they seek to follow the master in new and uncharted lands. Yet they remain faithful to his teaching, disciplining themselves even as they challenge others to convert and join them. So are we in approaching this revised code. We must not be timid in seeking a more creative approach to its implementation, to the development of those new wine skins that are so necessary if the nuance and promise of this code is to be captured. But true to the Lord's teaching, our new way of thinking must again lead us to that Gospel which is ever old and ever new, and out of whose treasures we continually seek to bring both the new and the old.

JAMES H. PROVOST, J.C.D.
Washington, D.C.

15

THE THREE-FOLD *MUNERA* OF CHRIST AND THE CHURCH

Canon 204 of the new law states that "the faithful participate in the priestly, prophetic and royal *munus* of Christ".

The word *munus* is difficult to translate: sometimes it is translated as "office" or "role", sometimes as "mission" or "service", and sometimes as "ministry", particularly in the United States, where the word "ministry" has taken on such a wide meaning. The doctrine of the three-fold *munera*, originally a Christology, was translated into an ecclesiology by the Second Vatican Council, and many of the documents of the council are structured in terms of these three offices or ministries. The Code of Canon Law has been similarly influenced by this doctrine.

Each of the three pivotal chapters of the Constitution on the Church, *Lumen gentium* treat of the three-fold *munera*.

Chapter Two—The People of God—presents the people of God as a priestly people. A distinction is made between the common priesthood of the faithful and the ministerial or hierarchial priesthood (*LG* 10-11). The people of God share in Christ's prophetic office. The whole body of the faithful cannot err in matters of belief; they have *"sensus fidei"*. Moreover, the people of God have special graces or charisms fitting them for their various tasks or offices (*LG* 12). Finally, the people of God are a kingdom, not of this earth (*LG* 13).

In Chapter Three on the Hierarchical Church, references to both the role of bishops and the role of presbyters are divided in accordance with the three-fold *munera*.

The bishops have a mission of teaching, wherein preaching the Gospel has pride of place (*LG* 24; 25). Bishops are stewards of the grace of the Supreme Priest. Churches, as Eucharistic communities, are presided over by bishops (*LG* 26). And the bishops govern the churches, having pastoral charge over them (*LG* 27). Similarly, presbyters are associated with bishops to preach the Gospel, to shepherd the faithful, and to celebrate divine worship (*LG* 28).

Finally, Chapter Four on the Laity is similarly structured. The laity share the priestly, prophetic and kingly office of Christ (*LG* 31). They have a priestly office (*LG* 34), they have a prophetic office and a responsibility to share in evangelization (*LG* 35), and the kingdom of justice, love and peace is spread by the lay faithful (*LG* 36).

The document on the role of bishops *Christus Dominus* further develops the concept of the three-fold *munera*: the bishop's teaching office, including preaching, catechetical instruction, doctrinal instruction in schools and public statements (*CD* 12; 13; 14); his sanctifying role (*CD* 15); and his pastoral role, including building community among the clergy, ecumenical dialogue, coordinating the apostolate, seeing to the special needs of people (*CD* 16-18).

Similarly, the document on presbyters deals with the three-fold office of a presbyter (*Presbyterorum ordinis*). The presbyter is a minister of God's Word (*PO* 4), a minister of the sacraments and the Eucharist (*PO* 5), and pastor and ruler of God's people (*PO* 6).

Finally, the document on the apostolate of the laity has a similar three-fold structure (*Apostolicam actuositatem*). The laity are made to share in the priestly, prophetical and kingly office of Christ (*AA* 2). The objectives of the lay apostolate include the apostolate of evangelization and sanctification (*AA* 6), the renewal of the temporal order (*AA* 7), and charitable works and social aid (*AA* 8). Moreover, the laity have a special role in church communities, acting as priest, prophet or king, taking part in parish and diocesan apostolates of evangelization, catechetical instruction and even assistance in the care of souls and the administration of church property (*AA* 10).

Two of the books in the new code, originally listed under *Res* in the 1917 Code, are now structured in accordance with the ecclesiological doctrine of the three *munera*, namely the book on the *munus docendi* (teaching mission), and the book on the *munus sanctificandi* (sanctifying mission). Even the Vatican Council was ambiguous regarding the significance of the *munus regendi* (governing mission). This *munus* includes the ministry of government, but is certainly not limited to that, since a reading of the Vatican II texts clearly shows that the *munus* includes the entire pastoral office and not just governance in the canonical sense. In fact, from the standpoint of the lay apostolate, the *munus* extends even to the transformation of the temporal order, and the Church's commitment to spiritual and corporal works of mercy. Because of this ambiguity, several reasons are given for neglecting a book on the *munus regendi*.

1. Since the *munus regendi* includes the ministry of governance, the entire code deals with the function or ministry.
2. From the standpoint of the lay apostolate and the transformation of social order, the *munus regendi* must be left to the particular church by reason of the doctrine of subsidiarity. It is only the particular church that can make adequate decisions regarding this aspect of the *munus regendi*.
3. Even interpreting the *munus regendi* as pastoral care suggests that much legislation needs to be left to the particular church, although one could say that the *munus regendi* is dealt with in many sections of Book Two on the People of God.
4. Finally, the *munus regendi* includes the administration of temporalities for the sake of worship, ministry, and the care of the poor, and from this point of view, Book Five on Church Property deals with some of the issues of this *munus regendi*.

BERTRAM F. GRIFFIN, J.C.D.
Portland, Oregon

THE AGES OF MAN

Jacques defines the seven ages of man as:
1. the infant, mewling and puking in the nurse's arms;
2. and then the whining school boy . . . creeping like snail, unwillingly, to school;
3. and then the lover, sighing like a furnace;
4. then a soldier, full of strange caths . . . seeking the bubble reputation, even in the cannon's mouth;
5. then the justice in fair round belly with good capon lined, . . . full of wise saws and modern instances;
6. in the sixth age, one shifts into the lean and slippered pantaloon, with spectacles on nose and pouch on side;
7. the last scene of all is second childishness and mere oblivion sans teeth, sans eyes, sans taste, sans everything.

(As You Like It, Act II, Scene 6,
Lines 140 and following)

The new Code on Canon Law, perhaps less descriptively, also speaks of seven ages of man: infants, children, youth, young adults, mature adults, older adults, and retired ministers.

1. Infants. Infancy extends until the age of reason, or discretion. One is presumed to have attained the age of reason at the age of seven (c. 97, §2). Infants are to be baptized within the first few weeks of life (c. 867, §1).

2. Children. Children are minors who are no longer infants, but who also do not have some of the rights of those young people who are still not considered adult. The age of childhood could be considered to stretch from the age of seven to the age of fourteen or sixteen. Certainly with the age of seven it is presumed that the child has left infancy.

Children who have reached the age of reason fall under the norms regarding adult baptism (c. 852, §1). The age of discretion is the usual age for confirmation, unless the episcopal conference decides on another age (c. 891). With the use of reason, children begin preparation for First Communion and celebrate First Communion as soon as they can (c. 914). Once children reach the age of discretion, they are required to confess their grave sins at least once a year (c. 989). Finally, with the use of reason, children can receive the sacrament of anointing of the sick (c. 1004, §1).

Having reached the use of reason, children can obtain a quasi-domicile (c. 105, §1). Infants and children under the age of fourteen follow the ritual transfer of their parents, but may return to the Latin Rite after that age (c.

111).

3. **Youth.** Youth could be said to begin with the age of fourteen or sixteen since special rights and obligations begin at those ages.

At the age of fourteen, one is free to choose one's own rite of baptism (c. 111, §2). Beginning with the age of fourteen, catechumens who wish to be baptized should be referred to the bishop (c. 863). Girls may validly marry at the age of fourteen; boys are restricted until the age of sixteen from valid marriage (c. 1083). With the age of fourteen, young people are bound by the law of abstinence (c. 1252).

At the age of sixteen, one can become a sponsor for baptism and confirmation (c. 874). With the age of sixteen, young people are bound by the law of ecclesiastical sanctions (c. 1323).

Prior to the age of eighteen, infants, children and young people (minors) are subject to their parents or tutors (c. 98) and retain the domicile and quasi-domicile of their parents or tutors (c. 105) (although, as we mentioned above, children over the age of seven can obtain their own quasi-domicile). Minors also must be represented before Church courts by their parents or tutors (c. 1478).

Prior to becoming adults at the age of eighteen, young people, even though capable of valid marriage, are still considered minors and may not marry if their parents are reasonably unwilling (c. 1071). Moreover, the episcopal conference can establish a higher are for liceity than the age of valid marriage (c. 1083, §2).

4. **Young Adults.** With the age of eighteen, one enters adulthood in the Church.

When one becomes an adult at the age of eighteen, one is bound to the law of fast on Ash Wednesday and Good Friday (c. 1252).

With the age of eighteen, one can make a valid temporary profession (c. 656) and therefore, must be at least seventeen years old for valid entrance into the novitiate of a religious institute (c. 643). Eighteen years is required for initial probation for entering a secular institute (c. 721) and commitments to a society of apostolic life cannot validly be made prior to the age of majority. Hence, young people may validly enter a novitiate at the age of seventeen (cc. 735 & 643).

With the age of eighteen, young adults can act as advocates or procurators in Church courts (c. 1483) and, as mentioned above, can stand in Church court on their own without parents or tutors (c. 1478).

5. **Mature Adults.** Certain rights and privileges can be exercised by adults who are somewhat more mature than the age of eighteen.

You may not make valid perpetual profession until the age of twenty-one.

You must be twenty-three years old before ordination to the transitional diaconate and twenty-five before ordination to the priesthood. You must be twenty-five before you can be ordained to the permanent celibate diaconate and thirty-five before the married permanent diaconate (c. 1031).

You must be thirty years old before you can be appointed a judicial vicar or an associate judicial vicar (c. 1420), a vicar general or an episcopal vicar (c. 478).

An you must be thirty-five years of age and at least five years as a presbyter before you can be nominated as a bishop (c. 378).

6. Older members of the Church. With the age of sixty, one is no longer obliged to fast (c. 1252).

Diocesan bishops are asked to submit their resignations at the age of seventy-five (c. 401) and pastors are also asked to submit their resignations at the age of seventy-five (c. 538).

Cardinals are also requested to submit their resignations at the age of seventy-five. However, once they reach the age of eighty, there are certain required limitations of their rights and prerogatives. They are required to retire as members of the Curia. The 1980 schema had reflected the present discipline that they are not permitted to participate in the election of a Pope, but the October, 1981 consultation recommended that this matter be referred to papal norms.

7. Retirement. This ends this strange, eventful history. I've been able to find no references in canon law to that "last scene of all—second childishness and mere oblivion—sans teeth, sans eyes, sans taste, sans everything"-—with the possible exception of those canons direction the episcopal conference to establish norms for the pensions of retired bishops (c. 402) and pastors (c. 538).

BERTRAM F. GRIFFIN, J.C.D.
Portland, Oregon

SOME RULES FOR GOVERNANCE[1]

It may be helpful to draw on the Church's tradition to sketch twelve "rules" or guidelines which may assist those in positions of governance.

1. Be always vigilant for the spiritual purpose of diocesan governance.

The salvation of souls is the supreme law of the Church. This is not only a literary device with which the legislator concluded the new code (c. 1752, at the end); it reflects the very purpose of diocesan governance, which is ultimately spiritual. Effective governance requires constant vigilance to the spiritual dimension of being Church.

2. Think with the Church.

Church law is to be interpreted in light of the teaching and new way of thinking characteristic of the Second Vatican Council.[2] *Sentire cum Ecclesia* is to resonate with the mystery of Christ as this is presented through the teaching, witness, and tradition of the Church. Diocesan governance steers not by the isolated lights of those currently at the helm, but by the wisdom of God made manifest in the Catholic communion as it carries out the mission entrusted to it.

3. Serve if you would lead.

Hierarchical authority is a service, directed toward the spiritual welfare of God's people.[3] This service of leadership implies the development of the personality of the leader, attention to the common good, and commitment to the spiritual goal for which the Church exists.

4. Use the power you have.

The bishop has all the power needed to exercise his pastoral office (c. 381, §1). There is no need, nor is it appropriate, to refer matters to a higher authority which properly pertain to the diocesan bishop as vicar and ambassador of Christ in the particular church. Failure to use power may not only be irresponsible, but damaging for the welfare of all the Church.

---

[1]From: "Canonical Reflection on Selected Issues in Diocesan Governance," James H. Provost in *The Ministry of Governance*, James K. Mallet, ed. (Washington, D.C.: Canon Law Society of America, 1986) 248-251.

[2]Paul VI, allocution to code commission, 20 November 1965: *AAS* 57 (1965) 988; John Paul II, allocution to Roman Rota, 26 January 1986: *AAS* 76 (1984) 645-646.

[3]See John Paul II, apostolic constitution *Sacrae disciplinae leges*, 25 January 1983: *AAS* 75, Part II (1983) xii.

5. Empower the Church.

All the Christian faithful, in virtue of Christ's action through the sacraments of initiation and charisms, participate in the mission which Christ gave the Church to accomplish in the world (c. 204, §1; *AA*, 3). To govern is to foster the common good; that is, to empower others to reach their potential, and thereby build up the Body of Christ.

6. Promote and protect rights.

The obligations and rights of Christians are the context in which the hierarchial structure of the Church performs its Christ-given ministry of service. They highlight the responsibility for which diocesan governance empowers Catholics in the communion and mission of the Church.

7. Consult when making decisions.

What touches all ought to be considered by all.[4] There is a standard pattern in the new code calling for consultation in coming to significant decisions. Sometimes this is required for validity (c. 127); otherwise, it is a general counsel for prudent action. Consulting also involves reminding those who have something to offer that they have an obligation to speak up (c. 127, §3), especially if they disagree.[5]

8. Interpret the law as it is meant to be interpreted.

Laws are made for God's people, not the people for laws. Indeed, no one is held to the impossible.[6] The laws are, therefore, not meant to be interpreted in such a way as to make Christian living impossible, nor to defeat the purpose of the salvation of souls. Any one who administers the law interprets it; a number of guides are available to help in this.[7]

9. Be generous.

The law itself is generous, even to an accused person: when there has been a change in the law, the law which is more favorable to the accused is to be applied (c. 1313, §1). Traditionally, favors are to be expanded and burden-

---

[4]*Regula Iuris [RI]* 29 in VI°: "Quod omnes tagit debet ab omnibus probari"; cited in *Commento al Codice di Diritto Canonico [Urbaniana]*, ed. Pio V. Pinto (Rome: Urbaniana University Press, 1985) 1031. See Yves Congar, "Quod Omnes Tangit, Ab Omnibus Tractari et Approbari Debet," *Revue historique de droit français et étranger* 35 (1958) 210-259.

[5]*RI* 43 in VI°: "Qui tacet consentire videtur"; cited in *Urbaniana*, 1031.

[6]*RI* 6 in VI°: "Nemo potest ad impossibile obligari"; cited in *Urbaniana*, 1031.

[7]See, for example, the studies by James A. Coriden, Richard A. Hill, Ellsworth Kneal and Ladislas Orsy, *The Art of Interpretation* (Washington: CLSA, 1982).

some matters restricted.[8] Moreover, laws which establish a penalty, restrict the free exercise of rights, or which contain an exception to the law are to be interpreted strictly (c. 18). On the other hand, the law is generous in situations of doubt.[9]

10. Be consistent.

Effective governance is governance people can count on. What once seemed proper ought not suddenly to be presented as improper,[10] nor should an opinion once adopted be changed to the detriment of another.[11] Indeed, legal consistency is a characteristic of the Church's legislation,[12] and should mark the service of those in diocesan governance.

11. Be timely.

If justice delayed is justice denied, so unnecessary delay in any aspect of governance can be harmful to people.[13] The code sets various time limits to enforce timely governance; even where no limits are specified, sensitivity to the rights of persons calls for prudent timeliness.

12. Be forthright.

The Church exists to bear witness to the gospel, to be a light to the nations. As with its teaching on social justice, so with forthrightness, the Church must practice what it preaches if it is to be a credible witness. Respecting proper confidentiality (c. 471) and preserving the privacy of others (c. 220) is important, but it cannot be an excuse for obscurantist practices or secretive governance. There is a standard pattern in the code encouraging forthrightness: norms require the promulgation of laws (c. 7), publication of judicial acts (c. 1598, §1), sentences (c. 1610), and administrative acts (c. 37). The truth, after all, has nothing to fear from being proclaimed.

JAMES H. PROVOST, J.C.D.
Washington, D.C.

[8]*RI* 15 in VI°: "Odia restringi et favores convenit ampliari"; cited in *Urbaniana*, 1031.

[9]When there is a doubt of law, even nullifying and disqualifying laws do not bind; in a doubt of fact, the possibility of dispensation exists (c. 14). In legal or factual common error, or a probable doubt about law or fact, the Church supplies executive power (c. 144, §1).

[10]*RI* 21 in VI°: "Quod semel placuit amplius displicere non potest"; cited in *Urbaniana*, 1031.

[11]*RI* 33 in VI°: "Mutare quis consilium non potest in alterius detrimentum"; cited in *Urbaniana*, 1031.

[12]See c. 21, and John Paul II in *Sacrae disciplinae leges, op. cit.*, xii, where he describes the new code as faithful in its newness and new in its fidelity.

[13]*RI* 25 in VI°: "Mora sua cuilibet nociva est"; *RI* 37 in VI°: "Utile per inutile non debet vitiari"; cited in *Urbaniana*, 1031.

PARTICULAR LEGISLATION

A. *What is particular legislation?*

A *law* is a general norm established for the common good of a specific community by competent authority.

When a law applies to the entire Latin Rite Church it is termed "universal"; when it applies to a smaller community, whether by territorial or by personal determination, it is termed "particular".

Promulgation is the moment when a law begins to exist.

B. *How is a particular law promulgated?*

The method of promulgation is left to the legislator (c. 8). If the legislator does not indicate the *vacatio legis* the law is understood to take effect one month from the moment of promulgation. Normally, the legislator should specify precisely when the law goes into effect. The *vacatio legis* for the 1983 Code was until November 27, 1983, the first Sunday of Advent.

C. *Who is a legislator in the Church?*

1. The Roman Pontiff and the College of Bishops possess full and supreme power in the Church (c. 331). Besides universal laws, the supreme authority of the Church may also pass laws which pertain only to certain territories or specific groups of Catholics. The American Procedural Norms were an example.

2. The diocesan bishop possesses legislative authority for the portion of God's people committed to his care (c. 391). Even when laws are formulated in a synod, the diocesan bishop is considered the sole legislator (c. 466).

3. Councils of bishops are also legislators in the Church:
   a. regional (national) councils (c. 439);
   b. provincial councils (c. 440).

In such councils all of the bishops who vote legislate collegially: diocesan bishops, coadjutor bishops, auxiliary bishops, and other active titular bishops. Retired bishops may also be called to council and vote (c. 443).

The decrees of the councils of bishops must be reviewed and recognized by Rome (c. 446).

4. Episcopal conferences may pass legislative decrees but are more restricted in doing so. They may do so only when the *"ius commune"* authorizes them or when they receive a petitioned or *motu proprio* mandate from the Apostolic See. In such matters, the law must be passed by two-thirds majority and be reviewed and recognized by Rome (c. 455).

5. The chapters of religious institutes are to pass laws which affect the members of the institute (c. 631). The particular law of a religious institute

24

is extremely important in the revised code. It consists in the institute's constitution and in its directory of statutes (c. 587).

D. *Who are bound by diocesan laws?*

Diocesan laws (and other particular laws) are presumed to be territorial in nature unless otherwise indicated. They bind therefore all of those who possess a domicile or quasi-domicile as long as they are actually present in the diocese (cc. 12-13).

Those visiting from another diocese are bound only by laws affecting public order, regulating the proper solemnities of acts, or affecting permanent structures (e.g., a sanctuary).

Those without any domicile or quasi-domicile are bound by all the particular laws of the diocese in which they find themselves.

E. *What forms to particular laws take in a diocese?*

1. Synodal laws (c. 460) are laws for the diocese.
2. General decrees are also laws and must be passed by the diocesan bishop himself (c. 29).
3. Customs become laws after being observed over a period of 30 years (c. 26).
4. General executory decrees can be passed by all with executive authority and may sometimes appear to be laws in themselves. More properly, they are detailed determinations of how laws are to be applied and observed. They are, however, promulgated and have a *vacatio legis* (c. 31).
5. Authoritative interpretation of a law can be given by the legislator and these are sometimes viewed as laws in themselves, particularly in a confusing matter (c. 16).
6. Most particular laws are disciplinary in nature (in the technical sense) but the diocesan bishop can also pass inhabilitating and irritating laws as well. In such cases the requisites or conditions for validity should be explicitly stated (cc. 14-15).
7. The legislator on the diocesan level may not delegate his legislative authority except in cases specified in law. Nevertheless, from a practical point of view, his reliance on consultation may often amount to the same thing (c. 135).
8. No law passed by a legislator with less than supreme authority may be contrary to laws passed by his superior. The same holds true for instructions which attempt to explain and draw out the meaning of higher laws. Insofar as they are contrary, they do not bind (c. 135; 34).
9. The phrase "particular law" is a very general one and many encompass many different types of norms with various authors and diverse levels of obligation. In drafting such norms, it is important to clarify these points as

much as possible.

F. *What are some models for drafting and passing particular law?*
1. The Executive Model
   Historically, many diocesan norms have resulted from this type of process. Administrators propose to the diocesan bishop various rules and regulations which are sent out to constituencies by letter.
   This can be an efficient method of producing needed norms. In general, however, this limited form of "professional" drafting should be limited to issues which are normally found in general executory decrees.
   One forum for this model might be found in the figure of the episcopal council mentioned in Book II (cc. 473; 407).
2. The Conciliar Model
   We have had much experience in drafting norms in the Vatican Council, in provincial councils and in the work of episcopal conferences. Theoretically, this is not done on the diocesan level since the diocesan bishop is the sole legislator but there is nothing to prevent a bishop from adopting this collegial style of action. The conciliar model draws together legislators and consultants from the entire people of God. It drafts and redrafts documents until a final form is achieved which wins a consensus. The rules for particular councils in the revised code are helpful in describing this experience. Not only are the various bishops convoked but the following are also called to council: vicars general and vicars episcopal; major superiors; rectors of Catholic universities and their deans of theology and canon law; rectors of seminaries. On the provincial level, there are also delegates of pastoral and presbyteral councils (c. 443).
3. The Synodal Model (cc. 460-468)
   The diocesan synod is the traditional canonical method of diocesan legislation. The revised code has changed little in this regard. In many ways, however, it shares the advantages of the conciliar model although in this case there is no deliberative voting since the bishop is seen as the sole legislator. Nevertheless, it is interesting to see the persons who must be called and can be called to participate in the diocesan synod (c. 463).
   Diocesan synods must be held only when the diocesan bishop, after consultation with the presbyteral council, judges them to be warranted by circumstances (c. 461). Their decrees are not sent to Rome (c. 467).
4. The Pastoral and Presbyteral Council Model
   The pastoral council is optional since the canons speak of its existence in dioceses in which pastoral conditions warrant it (c. 511).
   The presbyteral council and college of consultors are mandatory for all dioceses (c. 495).
   Both councils offer another style of drafting particular law through

representative consultation on a lesser scale than that of the synod. Both are strictly consultative in nature although a close working relationship between the bishop and his council(s) may in practice produce a broad model of governance, at least in the area of policy and norms (cc. 500; 514).

5. The Religious Chapter Model

Religious institutes have undergone a lengthy and sometimes painful juridical reorganization during the past decade or so. They have been involved in redrafting their constitutions and directories on a vast scale. As free associations of the faithful, they have had to discover many ways of eliciting the consensus of the community for the drafting of documents which would clarify their very identity and their basic structures of governance and discipline. Various institutes have approached this task in different ways. Canon lawyers can look upon religious who have shared this experience as valuable resources for guidance in developing particular law for the diocese by pointing the way to successful processes of drafting law.

6. The Revision of the Code Model

Since the Vatican Council we have seen the code of universal laws revised and redrafted. The process involved:

    a.   initial groups to develop primary drafts of revised law;
    b.   widespread consultation with bishops, major superiors and academic groups;
    c.   small groups collating animadversions, consulting and revising the primary drafts;
    d.   written animadversions and revisions in dialogue with an international commission;
    e.   plenary sessions of the international commission;
    f.   individual consultation by the pope and the commission staff in the final stages.

This model might be fruitful in constructing a diocesan method of drafting particular law without requiring the convocation of large gatherings.

JOHN A. ALESANDRO, J.C.D.
Rockville Centre, New York

THE RIGHTS AND OBLIGATIONS OF CLERICS

I. Introduction

The canons which deal with the rights and obligations of the clergy are rooted in the documents of the Second Vatican Council, principally *Lumen gentium*, Chapter III, *Christus Dominus*, Chapter II, and *Presbyterorum ordinis*, the entire document. Although Chapter III of Book II deals with the rights and obligations of clerics as clerics, there are rights and obligations which are applicable to clerics in virtue of their office as pastors and associate pastors (Book II, Chapter IX, which should be discussed under the same title). In any case, the above-mentioned documents together with the early *motu proprios*, must notably *Ecclesiae Sanctae*, should be restudied before beginning a commentary on these canons.

The code accepts the basic conciliar definition of the Church as "the people of God" and legislates Church mission and ministry within the context of a hierarchical communion (*Lumen gentium*, Chapt. III, n. 18).

Although the code emphasizes the authority of clergy, particularly bishops and presbyters, they are directed to honor the charisma of lay persons and invite their collaboration in the work of Church ministry (cc. 129; 275, §2; 517, §2; 529, §1; 1421, §2).

The Church of Vatican II is clearly reflected in the code. Yet in many respects the pastoral practice of the Church has progressed beyond the notions espoused at the council. Any commentary on the new code, therefore, will be inadequate without theological reflection on present pastoral practice since the close of the Second Vatican Council. While it is true the code has solidified certain definitions and structures and determined the rights and roles of certain persons in the Church, the code nevertheless leaves room for the application of recent insights into the mission and ministry of the Church. An example of this may be seen in canon 528, §1 in which pastors are encouraged to become involved in the promotion of social justice. It is hardly more than an honorable mention. Nevertheless, it is becoming clear from the recent practice of the American bishops, the work of social justice plays a major role in the life of the pastoral leader. This factor has created a significant increase in literature and commentary on the appropriate role of the clergy in social issues. This issue also touches upon the degree to which a priest may become involved in politics (cc. 285, §§2-3; 287, §2).

Institutions, codes and systems are established to help people become more than they could become without those institutions. When systems cripple people psychologically or spiritually, they must be evaluated and, if necessary, changed so that the members of the institution can freely commit themselves to its ideals and goals. Church processes, systems, and institutions are not ends in themselves. They are intended to enable people to move toward wholeness and salvation.

People are the most valuable resource of any institution. Presbyters, in particular, are a most valuable, indeed, an essential resource within the Church. Decisions made at the diocesan level should encourage and foster the growth of the presbyterate as much as the growth of the people of God within the diocesan church.

Presbyters possess the same basic human needs as those of lay persons—physical security, a sense of belonging, self-esteem, and a share in determining their destiny. Institutions are challenged today to provide an environment in which these basic human needs can be addressed. Presbyters also share in the obligations and rights of all the Christian faithful (cc. 208-223).

At the same time, it must be recognized that these needs cannot be fully met this side of the parousia. Moreover, concentration on self to the exclusion of others can only lead to selfism and disillusionment. Yet, it must be admitted that people do mature when they take serious responsibility for their life and actions. When a person has little or no control over his life, he remains immature and tends to treat others in a like manner, exceptions notwithstanding.

The Church should be in the vanguard in promoting that spiritual freedom which enables its members to offer a total "yes" to God in imitation of His Son, who was obedient to the Father in all things, even death itself. It is a holy paradox that those who have the greatest potential for obedience to the will of God are those who are most spiritually free, aided, of course, by divine grace. The code then, can only set minimal standards which govern and guide the external behavior of its members, especially the clergy.

In the Rite of Ordination of Priests, the ordaining bishop reminds candidates for the priesthood and the faithful assembly that "presbyters are co-workers of the college of bishops since they are joined to bishops in the priestly office and are called to serve the people of God".

As principal pastor of the diocesan church, the bishop has a primary concern for all the people of God entrusted to him. His position is not one of honor, but of service. It is his sensitive responsibility to discern with his brother priests how their gifts and charisms can be used most effectively in meeting the pastoral needs of that portion of the people of God called the diocesan church. His love for his brother priests can be no less than his love for all the people. They are his "partners in the ministry of Christ" (Rite of Ordination for Bishops). Therefore, it is his challenge to collaborate with them in such a way that they, too, will mature in their love for God and neighbor. "I must distinguish carefully," says St. Augustine, "between two aspects of the role the Lord has given me, a role that demands a rigorous accountability, a role based on the Lord's greatness rather than on my own merit. The first aspect is that I am a Christian; the second, that I am a leader for your sake; the fact that I am a Christian is to my own advantage, but I am a leader for your advantage . . . as a leader I must give Him [God] an account of my stewardship."

The instruction contained in the Rite of Ordination concludes with a plea to work in union and harmony with the bishop and try to bring the faithful together like a unified family so that they may be led effectively through Christ and in the Holy Spirit of God the Father. The clergy are urged to remember the example of the good shepherd who came to serve rather than be served.

Although the new code may only move the Church officially from a Vatican I to a Vatican II definition of the Church, it does not deny the dynamism that must be part of a living organism.

Consequently, the prudent practitioner of the law will be a wise counselor who is able to bring out of the code both new things and old, which honor the tradition and recognize the power of the Spirit guiding the growth and development of the Church into the future.

II. Rights and Obligations of Clergy

A. *Rights of Clergy*
1.   Only the clergy can assume offices which require the power of orders (c. 274).

Although the law allows deacons and lay persons to participate in pastoral ministry due to the shortage of priests (c. 517, §2), only a priest can be appointed to the full pastoral care of souls (c. 150).

The revised code also gives stability to the office of pastor who must be a priest. His appointment is for an indefinite period of time (c. 522).

2.   Secular clerics have the right to join with others in the pursuit of goals that conform to the clerical state (c. 278, §1).

3.   Right to an adequate income in remuneration for the fulfillment of their ministry. This income should be commensurate with their position, adequate for their necessities, and sufficient for the cleric to give an equitable income to those whose services he may require in the fulfillment of his responsibilities (c. 281, §1) Permanent deacons are treated as a separate case (c. 281, §3).

4.   Right to social assistance which will provide for their necessities in time of illness, incapacity, or old age (c. 281, §2).

5.   Right to a reasonable period of vacation (c. 283, §2).

Pastors and associate pastors are entitled to one month's vacation (cc. 533, §2; 550, §3).

B. *General Obligations for Clergy*

1.   Unless legitimately prevented, clerics are bound to assume and faithfully fulfill the assignment given to them by their ordinary (c. 274, §2).

2.   May not be absent from the diocese for a notable period of time without at least the presumed permission of one's own ordinary (c. 283, §1).

3.   Bound by a special obligation to reverence and obedience to the Holy Father and to his own ordinary (c. 273).

4.   As consecrated in a special way to God and as dispensers of God's mysteries in the service of the people of God, clerics are obliged to seek spiritual perfection in their own lives (c. 276, §1).

5.   Bound by daily recitation of the Divine Office (c. 276, §2, 3°).

6.   Obligated to undertake spiritual retreats in accord with local regulations (c. 276, §2, 4°).

7.   Bound to celibacy (c. 277, §1).

8.   Act prudently in their habitual association with persons when such association can endanger celibacy or cause scandal (c. 277, §2).

9.   Avoid groups or associations whose goals and activities are not in conformity with clerical obligations or interfere with the fulfillment of their priestly responsibilities (c. 278, §3).

10. Continue sacred studies, follow the solid teaching based on scripture, handed down in tradition, accepted by the Church and set forth especially in documents of the councils and popes, avoiding innovations based on worldly novelty and false knowledge (c. 279, §1).

11. In accordance with local law, participate in continuing education courses and conferences with the aim of acquiring a greater knowledge of the theological sciences and pastoral methods necessary to fulfill priestly responsibilities (c. 279, §2).

12. Wear suitable ecclesiastical attire in accord with norms of the episcopal conference and local custom (c. 284).

13. Completely avoid whatever is unbecoming to their state of life in accord with local norms (c. 285, §1).

14. Avoid those things which, though not unbecoming in themselves, are inconsistent with the priestly state (c. 285, §2).

15. Forbidden to assume public office, especially one which involves the exercise of civil power, without permission of both the proper bishop and the bishop of the place where he intends to exercise administrative authority (c. 285, §3).

16. Without permission of the bishop, priests may not undertake the administration of property which belongs to lay persons or to assume a secular office which requires the duty of rendering an account; also forbidden to offer bail even upon security of his own property without consulting the ordinary. Priests are also forbidden to sign a surety for an obligation to pay money (c.

285, §4).

17. Forbidden, without permission of legitimate ecclesiastical authority, to conduct business or trade either personally or through others, for personal gain or for the benefit of others (c. 286).

18. May not take an active role in political factions or in the management of labor unions unless, in the judgment of the competent ecclesiastical authority and with its permission, it would be required for the protection of the rights of the Church and for the common good (c. 287, §2).

19. May not enter military service without permission of the bishop (c. 289, §1).

20. Are to take advantage of civil laws exempting them from duties and public offices foreign to the clerical state (c. 289, §2).

21. As cooperators with the bishop, priests have the duty to proclaim the gospel of God (c. 757).

22. Priests must regard preaching as a priority inasmuch as their primary responsibility is the proclamation of the gospel to everyone (c. 762).

23. Priests must see to it with zeal that they stir up and teach the Christian faith, especially through the ministry of the Word (c. 836).

24. Priests have the obligation to give the sacraments to the faithful who are properly disposed and are not prohibited by law from receiving them (c. 843, §1).

25. Priests are obliged to give the sacraments only to Catholics and are forbidden to give them to non-Catholics except in circumstances permitted in the law (c. 844, §1).

26. Permanent deacons are not bound by the requirements of canon 284; 285, §§3 and 4; 286; 287, §2 (i.e., numbers 12, 15, 16, 17, 18 above).

C. *Responsibilities of Pastors*

1. Pastor is bound by the obligation of providing that the Word of God be proclaimed integrally to all in the parish. This is emphasized in several canons as a primary duty not of pastors but of all priests with the care of souls (cc. 528, §1; 702).

2. As part of the duty of announcing the Word of God, the pastor must see to it that the faithful are taught the truths of the faith (c. 528, §1).

3. One of the chief obligations the pastor has in teaching the truths of the faith is to see to it that homilies are given at least on Sundays and days of precept (cc. 528, §1; 767, §4).

4. The pastor has a grave duty to provide catechetical instruction to all of the people committed to his care. This catechesis is to be provided for adults and in a special way to children and the young. In this important responsibility, the pastor is to utilize the resources of other priests, religious, and laity (cc. 528, §1; 773; 776-777).

5. Pastors must also strive with every effort to bring the gospel message to the faithful who may have fallen away from belief in a practice of the faith (cc. 528, §1; 771, §1).

6. Pastors also should be solicitous of bringing the evangelical message to non-believers in his parish (cc. 528, §1; 771, §2).

7. Pastors have the duty of making available the means whereby all the faithful may receive a Catholic education (cc. 528, §1; 794, §2).

8. Pastors must also support activities in which the spirit of the gospel and what concerns social justice are promoted (c. 528, §1).

9. Paraphrasing Vatican II, the revised code calls on the pastor to make the Eucharist the center of the life of the parish, especial through frequent reception of Communion and penance, through family prayer, through participation in the Sacred Liturgy which he, under the authority of the bishop, should regulate and ensure that no abuses occur (c. 528, §1).

10. Again borrowing from the Vatican II decrees as well as from the 1917 Code, the revised code urges the pastor to know his people, visit their homes, share in their concerns, anxieties and especially in their grief at the time of death, comforting them; in time of failure, correcting them prudently; assisting the sick, especially those near death; solicitously comforting them with the sacraments and commending their souls to God (c. 529, §1).

11. It is the duty of the pastor to acknowledge and support the proper role which the laity have in the mission of the Church, promoting their associations which have religious purposes (c. 529, §2).

12. Pastor must cooperate with the bishop and the diocesan presbyterate in striving to achieve parish community. He must bring the people to the point where they see themselves also as members of the diocese and of the universal Church (c. 529, §2).

13. As in the present law, the revised code lists certain functions of the pastor. While in the 1917 Code is calls them functions reserved to the pastor, the revised code is more realistic and describes them as functions entrusted to the pastor. They are the following (c. 530):

  a. Administration of baptism. In the 1917 Code, solemn baptism is reserved to the pastor.

  b. Administration of confirmation to the dying. This faculty is not in the 1917 Code though pastors have had this faculty for many years.

  c. Administration of Viaticum, anointing of the sick, imparting of an apostolic blessing. In the 1917 Code, it is carrying Viaticum that is reserved. Similarly reserved in the 1917 Code is carrying the Eucharist publicly to the sick. This reserved function was repeated in the schema of the new code but removed in the final revision of October, 1981.

  d. Assist at marriages and impart the nuptial blessing. Omitted in the revised code is the reserved function of announcing the banns for ordinations and marriages.

e. Perform funeral services.

f. Bless the baptismal font at Holy Saturday services, leading processions outside the church, giving solemn blessings outside the church.

g. More solemn celebration of Eucharist on Sundays and days of precept. This function is new and is not in the 1917 Code. Omitted in the new code is the 1917 Code's reserved function of blessing homes on Holy Saturday.

14. In all juridical transactions, the pastor acts in the name of the parish. He must take care, therefore, that he administer the property of the Church in accord with canonical norms (c. 532).

15. The pastor is obliged to reside in a parish house near the church. The bishop can permit him to reside elsewhere, especially in a residence with other priests, provided he can still carry out his parochial functions adequately (c. 533, §1).

16. The pastor is obliged to offer the *Missa pro populo* for his parish on Sundays and days of precept. If impeded, he is to do so on other days or through some other priest (c. 534, §1). In the 1917 Code, the number of Masses was about 88. Over the years, the list was simplified until the norm of the revised code which limits the obligation to Sundays and days of precept.

17. The pastor has the responsibility of providing and assiduously maintaining parish registers for baptism, marriage, and the dead. While the schema also called for a confirmation register, this requirement was eliminated in the final revision of October, 1981 and it is now left to local law to determine if necessary (c. 535, §1).

18. The pastor must also see to it that all required annotations be placed in the baptismal register (c. 535, §2).

19. Pastors must keep a parochial seal (c. 535, §3).

20. Pastors must maintain archives in which are to be kept the parish registers as well as letters from the bishop and other important documents (c. 535, §4).

21. If the bishop judges it useful, the pastor must establish a parish pastoral council over which he presides (c. 536, §1).

22. Pastors must have a parish finance council utilizing the laity to help in the administration of parish property (c. 537).

23. Pastors, in accord with diocesan norms, should at regular intervals hold retreats or missions or other spiritual exercises adapted to the needs of the parish (c. 770).

24. The pastor has responsibility to keep custody of the holy oils obtained from the bishop (c. 847, §2).

25. The pastor has a special obligation concerning the sacrament of

matrimony. He is obliged to see to it that his ecclesial community gives support to the faithful so that the marital state is maintained in the Christian spirit and grows toward perfection. The code then suggests some methods that he could utilize to achieve this important goal (c. 1063).

D. *Responsibilities of Associate Pastors*

There are very few canons on the rights and obligations of associate pastors, referred to in the code as "parochial vicars". Inasmuch as they are collaborators of the pastor, with few exceptions what applies to pastors also applies to associate pastors.

1. When appointed the associate pastor becomes the cooperator with the pastor in the pastoral care of the parish but under his authority (c. 545, §1).

2. The details of obligations of the associate pastor are left to diocesan regulations, the letter of appointment by the bishop, and especially to the instructions given to the associate by the pastor (cc. 548, §1; 545, §1).

3. The associate pastor is obliged to assist the pastor in carrying out the pastoral ministry to the whole parish, excluding the application of the *Missa pro populo*. When circumstances warrant it, the associate pastor takes the place of the pastor (c. 548, §2).

E. *Exhortations*

1. Since all clerics are working together to achieve the same goal, the building up of the Body of Christ, they should be united among themselves in a bond of fraternity and prayer and should strive for cooperation with each other in accord with local law (c. 275, §1).

2. Clerics should recognize and promote the mission which the laity exercise in the Church and in the world (c. 275, §2).

3. Among the means clerics may utilize in striving for spiritual perfection in their own lives, the following are recommended:
    a. First of all, faithfully and zealously fulfilling their pastoral ministry;
    b. Reading of scripture;
    c. Reception of the Eucharist; especially urged is daily celebration of Mass;
    d. Meditation;
    e. Frequent confession;
    f. Devotion to the Blessed Virgin Mary;
    g. Other means of sanctification (c. 276, §2).

4. Especially valuable for secular clerics are those societies or associations which afford a fraternal support, encourage holiness in the priestly ministry, and promote fraternal unity among priests and with the bishop (c. 278, §2).

5. Should study even non-sacred sciences especially those related to the sacred sciences, particularly if they help in the pastoral ministry (c. 279, §3).

6. Strongly recommended is some form of community life for clerics. Where it exists, it should be maintained (c. 280).

7. Clerics should cultivate a simplicity of life and shun anything that smacks of worldliness (c. 282, §1).

8. Exhorts clerics to give any surplus funds they may have after providing for their own necessities, to the activities of the Church and to charitable causes (c. 282, §2).

9. Should promote as much as possible the preservation of peace and harmony among all people (c. 287, §1).

KENNETH E. LASCH, J.C.D.
Paterson, New Jersey

SUPRA-DIOCESAN STRUCTURES[1]

After an introductory summary on the successors of Peter and of the apostles (c. 330), the canons on supreme authority are divided into five chapters. The first deals with the subjects of supreme authority, i.e., the Roman Pontiff (cc. 331-335) and the college of bishops (cc. 336-341). Ecumenical councils are dealt with as an expression of episcopal collegiality in keeping the *Lumen gentium* 22. The remaining four chapters address specific agencies through which the exercise of supreme authority is carried out on a more frequent or regular basis in the Church universal: the synod of bishops (cc. 342-348), cardinals of the Holy Roman Church (cc. 349-359), the Roman Curia (cc. 360-361), and legates of the Roman Pontiff (cc. 362-367).

THE ROMAN PONTIFF AND THE COLLEGE OF BISHOPS

The relationship of pope and college of bishops is based on the relationship the Lord established between Peter and the other apostles. Vatican II taught that the Lord constituted the apostles as a stable body or college and selected Peter from among their number as head of the group. The introductory canon (c. 330) is a statement about both the college of bishops and the primacy of the pope, basing the foundation for their roles in the Church on the extent to which bishops are successors of the apostles and the pope is the successor of Peter. The source of this canon is *Lumen gentium* 22.

The canon therefore proposes that the relationship of the Roman Pontiff to the rest of the bishops is similar to that which existed between Peter and the rest of the apostles: they constitute, by the Lord's will, one single college that continues the mission given to the apostolic college. Within the college of bishops, the pope continues the functions that Peter had among the apostles. The pope does not succeed to the role Christ had vis à vis the apostles but to that which Peter was given within the group.

Papal primacy is a function entrusted to the office of Peter and his successors for building up the Church: it is pastoral in nature. It is exercised in an ecclesial context; hence, it is essentially a relationship in communion for safeguarding the unity of the Church and providing for the effective exercise of the Church's mission.

---

[1]Précis of commentary, Provost, James H., "Section I: Supreme Church Authority (cc. 330-367)" in *The Code of Canon Law: A Text and Commentary*, ed. James A. Coriden, et al. (New York/Mahwah: Paulist Press, 1985) 260-310.

While it means that the pope can intervene in any case, at any time, or in any place in the Church for the purpose of the pastoral life and welfare of the people of God, it does not make the pope a "super bishop" or replace the role of bishops and others in the Church. Instead, it is meant to affirm, strengthen, and safeguard their offices.

The pope is mentioned specifically in reference to a number of issues. For example, clergy are bound to special obedience toward him (c. 273), and religious are held to obey him in virtue of the vow of obedience (c. 590, §2). The pope may celebrate the sacraments, including penance (c. 967, §1) anywhere; he may dispense private vows of anyone, anywhere (c. 1196); appeal to him at any stage of a process is always permitted in virtue of his primacy (c. 1417, §1). Indeed, he is the supreme judge for the whole Catholic world (c. 1442).

The pope has a special role in the acts of the college of bishops (cc. 337-338; 341) and in admitting new members to the college through the nomination of bishops or the confirmation of their election (c. 377). Bishops are to report to him every five years on their ministry in pastoring a diocese (c. 399, §1), and he can send legates of his own to any place or person. Through his primatial power the pope can limit the competence of diocesan bishops, reserving certain matters to himself or other authorities (c. 381, §1) or exempting religious from the bishop's authority (c. 591).

In virtue of the primacy, the pope is supreme administrator and dispenser of ecclesiastical goods (c. 1273), and those who exercise the right of ownership over church goods always do so under his authority (c. 1256).

Dispensing clergy from celibacy is restricted to the pope (c. 291), as is dispensation from a ratified but not consummated marriage (cc. 1142; 1698, §2). The judgment of certain cases is reserved to him (c. 1405, §2).

The Roman Pontiff is aided in the exercise of his office by other members of the college of bishops, particularly through certain institutions and groups.

The college of bishops exercises the supreme power of the Church in several ways. In a strictly collegial act it does so solemnly when gathered in an ecumenical council and in a less solemn manner when dispersed throughout the world. As its head the pope has the responsibility to determine in which manner the college will act, and both types of action require the involvement not only of the members themselves of the college but also of the head of the college who either initiates the action or freely accepts it.

ECUMENICAL COUNCILS

Ecumenical councils are the most solemn assemblies in the Christian world. Vatican II is considered by the Catholic reckoning to be the twenty-first ecumenical council. The first four (Nicaea, Constantinople I, Ephesus, and

38

Chalcedon) are generally recognized as normative by all orthodox Christians of East and West, and indeed in many ways constitute the touchstone of orthodoxy in ecumenical relations.

SYNOD OF BISHOPS

The "synodal principle" is an ancient one in the Church. It means that people come together to discuss major issues in the Church and at times make practical determinations about those issues. The principle is applied analogously in different settings. An ecumenical council is a "synod". So, too, are particular councils, diocesan synods, and today, special bodies of bishops which meet with the pope to review issues of major significance to the Church universal.

The present "synod of bishops" is an innovation from the Second Vatican Council. Some have seen it roots in the "permanent synods" held in former times by some of the Oriental Patriarchates, especially Constantinople, but its more immediate cause was the experience of free and open discussion on issues of considerable importance in the presence of the pope. This began with the meetings of the preparatory commissions for Vatican II when a new spirit began to be felt even among the bishops in the Church, a spirit of dialogue and honest searching for pastorally effective approaches to the issues of the times.

THE CARDINALS OF THE HOLY ROMAN CHURCH

The cardinals are a unique feature of Roman Catholicism. They exercise major influence in the Church, not only because they form the college that elects the bishop of Rome, but also because they occupy major positions in the central administration of the Church and increasingly, are the diocesan bishops of major sees around the world.

"Cardinal" comes from the Latin word for hinge (*cardo*). A hinge has a double function. It serves as a pivot on which, for example, a door swings in a doorjamb; it also attaches the door (something from outside the doorjamb itself) to the wall.

Three major functions of cardinals are described in canon 349. First and specific to them is the duty of electing the bishop of Rome. They also provide a special advisory body that the pope can call on to deal with questions of major importance. Finally, they individually assist the pope in various ways—but particularly in performing special offices (such as in the Roman Curia) for the daily care of the universal Church.

Cardinals provide their advise to the pope collegially in consistories (c. 353) and collectively in general meetings of the cardinals; they also head various offices of the Roman Curia or serve on the various congregations of the Curia even if their full-time responsibility is to pastor a particular church elsewhere in the world.

The Roman Curia is composed of the various offices and related services that assist the supreme authority of the Church in its ministry of service and governance in the Church.

Canon 360 describes the Curia as the instrument through which the pope usually conducts the business of the universal Church. Drawing on the words of *Christus Dominus* 9, it indicates that the Curia exists for the good and the service of the particular churches that form the communion of the universal Church. The chief categories of dicasteries are named, and reference is made to particular law for the structure and competence of these offices. The particular law regulating the Roman Curia was reformed by Pope John Paul II in his apostolic constitution *Pastor Bonus*.

Secretariat of State

If an organizational chart were to be drawn of the Roman Curia, the Secretariat of State would appear as the chief middle manager in the Curia. The Secretariat of State is responsible for aiding the pope in his relationships with the universal Church and in dealing with the other departments of the Roman Curia. It is responsible for coordinating the work of the various curial offices, and regular meetings of the heads of the dicasteries are presided over by the Secretary of State. Matters not clearly within the competence of one or another dicastery are handled by the Secretariat. In principle, direct access to the pope himself is through the Secretariat. Together with the Council for the Public Affairs of the Church, the Secretariat supervises the work of papal legates around the world.

Congregations

The congregations have a distinctive organization. Technically the "congregation" consists in the committee of cardinals and bishops who are charged with the responsibility of caring for a particular concern on behalf of the supreme authority of the Church and in service to the churches. Each congregation is chaired by a "prefect," called a "pro-prefect" if he is not a cardinal, who is assisted by a secretary (usually a titular archbishop) and a staff of varying proportions.

The cardinal prefect, secretary, and major staff personnel meet frequently to carry on the ordinary business of dicastery within the policy set by the plenary session and in keeping with decisions reached in the ordinary

40

meetings. This group, known as the *congressus*, also decides what to do with issues that are brought to the congregation's attention: whether to submit them to the pope directly, to place them on the agenda for a plenary session, or to handle them in an ordinary session. The congregations draw on experts in their respective fields, usually from among those living in Rome but also calling on the help of others around the world.

Tribunals

There are three tribunals as part of the Roman Curia. Each has a unique organization.

1. *Apostolic Penitentiary.* The Penitentiary grants favors, absolutions, dispensations, commutations, sanctions, and condonations for the internal forum.

2. *Supreme Tribunal of the Apostolic Signatura.* This is the supreme court of the external forum in the Church, and exercises vigilance over the tribunals of the particular churches.

3. *The Roman Rota.* The word "rota" is the Latin word for wheel and is applied to this court, the main appellate court of the Roman Curia, because of the system for determining the composition of various panels of judges (or *ternus*). The Rota also has its own special rules of procedure, and is most frequently involved with marriage cases on appeal from local tribunals.

THE LEGATES OF THE ROMAN PONTIFF

The Roman Pontiff as a spiritual leader has the right to use legates in his relationships with local churches and with civil governments, without any other power having the right to interfere with this activity. The only limitations recognized by canon law are the norms of international law.

The right of the Roman Pontiff to send legates is said to be innate, that is, it comes with the office rather that as something conceded by other (e.g., civil) authorities to the pope. The basis for this international role of the Holy See is its worldwide spiritual mission—making it an international entity with a different nature than that of a civil government but giving the Holy See a genuine standing in international law. The diplomatic relations of the pope are always carried on in light of this spiritual mission, hence legates represent the Holy See—not the State of Vatican City; civil governments enter into relations not with the State of Vatican City but with the Holy See itself. Even the title given representatives of the Holy See ("nuncios" rather than "ambassadors") is intended to underscore the particular nature of their mission.

NATIONAL CHURCH STRUCTURES

THE EPISCOPAL CONFERENCE

The revised code devotes thirteen canons to the episcopal conference. This conference has a major role in the local church as a clearing house for ideas and policies. The episcopal conference is a planning institute on a national level for pastoral activity and the apostolate. Hence, the episcopal conference will exercise a lot of its role in terms of pastoral coordination, the publication of directories, the development of consensus, and the undertaking of regional projects.

Still, there are many explicit references to the episcopal conference's influence on the local level in terms of particular law. The following is not meant to be a complete list of all the specific references to the episcopal conference and the new law, but like the catalogues in *Finnegan's Wake*, can give a feeling for the extent of the episcopal conference's influence in Church life.

Regarding ministry

The episcopal conference establishes norms for the formation and training of permanent deacons (c. 236) and norms for the training of priests and for the *Ratio Studiorum* (c. 242).

The episcopal conference can erect a national seminary with the approval of the Holy See and approve its statutes (c. 237, §2).

The episcopal conference can establish norms on clerical dress (c. 284).

The episcopal conference establishes the age and qualifications for the installed ministries of lector and acolyte (c. 230).

Regarding the diocese

The episcopal conference establishes norms and provides for the pension of retired bishops (c. 402, §2) and norms for the pensions of pastors (c. 538, §3).

The episcopal conference can establish norms for the council of presbyters (c. 496).

The episcopal conference can permit a term of office for pastors (c. 522).

The episcopal conference can establish norms for parish records over and above those for baptism, marriage, and the deceased (c. 535, §1).

Regarding the teaching office

The conference can establish norms:

for promoting participation in the ecumenical movement (c. 755, §2);

for the reception of penance, Eucharist and the anointing of the sick by baptized non-Catholics in cases of necessity (c. 844);

42

for lay preaching (c. 766), for radio and TV preaching (c. 772, §2); for religious education in schools and on the radio or TV (c. 775);

for participation of clerics and religious in radio and TV programs regarding Catholic doctrine and morality (c. 831, §2).

With the approval of the Holy See the episcopal conference may publish a national catechism (c. 775) and set up a national catechetical office to assist dioceses in the region.

The episcopal conference establishes norms for the ordering of the catechumenate and determines the rights and obligations of catechumens (c. 788). Interestingly enough, in number 14 of the Decree of Missionary Activity *Ad gentes*, Vatican II states: "The juridical status of catechumens should be clearly defined in the new Code of Canon Law." The new code, on the principle of subsidiarity, relegates the juridical status of catechumens to the episcopal conference, apparently on the assumption that the rights and obligations of catechumens and their status in the Church will differ from continent to continent and nation to nation.

Finally, the episcopal conference should be responsible for the distribution of universities and Catholic faculties (c. 809), and higher institutions of religious studies (c. 821).

Regarding the liturgy

The episcopal conference can issue norms in regard to sacramental ministry in an ecumenical context, namely, sacraments of penance, Eucharist, and anointing of the sick for non-Catholics in danger of death or other grave need (c. 844, §4).

The episcopal conference also has extensive influence over the catechumenate, as mentioned above. The conference sees to preparation of vernacular translations of liturgical books (c. 838, §3); can adapt the *Ordo Initiationis* (c. 851), and issue special liturgical norms in this area. Again, as an interesting sidelight, the new code suggests that fourteen year olds and older should be referred to the bishop for baptism. A restriction was also in the 1917 Code of Canon Law, but for sixteen year olds. In the United States, all pastors and generally all priests have faculties to baptize adults.

The episcopal conference can issue norms regarding the celebration of the sacrament of baptism by infusion and immersion (c. 854).

Although the normal age for confirmation is the age of discretion, the episcopal conference can establish a different age (c. 891).

The episcopal conference can establish norms for the confessional and attached grill (c. 964).

The episcopal conference has extensive influence in the area of marriage preparation. It can establish norms regarding the pre-nuptial inquiries and the banns (c. 1067). The age for valid celebration of marriage is fourteen for girls and sixteen for boys in the new code. The episcopal conference can establish a higher age for the licit celebration of marriage (c. 1083) although it cannot establish an invalidating impediment. The episcopal conference can establish norms for the ritual of marriage (c. 1120), for the registration of marriage (c. 1121), and for the mixed marriage promises (c. 1126).

In the revised Code of Canon Law the holy days of obligation are retained, but the episcopal conference can abolish or transfer some of them to the nearest Sunday (c. 1246, §2).

The episcopal conference can also establish additional rules on abstinence or provide for the substitution of other kinds of works (cc. 1251 and 1253).

REGARDING OTHER MATTERS

For *financial matters* the conference establishes norms for support of the Church (c. 1262), norms for other fund raising events (c. 1265), social security for the clergy not provided by civil society, norms for leasing church property. The episcopal conference also establishes a maximum and minimum sum for the alienation of stable patrimony (c. 1292). In *tribunal matters* the episcopal conference may permit a single judge in first instance (c. 1425), may set up regional appeal courts (c. 1439), and can require every diocese to set up a conciliation office or panel (due process) (c. 1733).

THE PLENARY COUNCIL

The episcopal conference is not basically a legislative body. Legislation on the national level or its equivalent is done by a plenary council. The episcopal conference has legislative power only on two occasions: when canon law prescribes it (for example, the conference must decide whether to convoke a plenary council); and secondly, when mandated by the Holy See. The Holy See may mandate such legislative activity at the request of the conference, or the Holy See itself may take the initiative. Legislation enacted by the conference must be passed by a two-thirds majority of the membership in these cases; otherwise, if the episcopal conference wishes to pass legislation in cases other than the two above, unanimous consent is required.

The plenary council is a council of all the particular churches in the territory (i.e., dioceses). The episcopal conference decides on the frequency of the plenary council, convokes it, selects a site, sets the agenda, and opens and closes the council. The members of the plenary council are the same as the episcopal conference; other members can, and some must, be invited with consultative vote, including both priests and lay people (c. 443). The decisions of the plenary council bind the local bishop. For special pastoral reasons, as is always the case in church law, the local bishop can dispense from appropriate decrees in his own diocese.

NATIONAL PASTORAL COUNCIL

In the revised code there is no consultative pastoral council on the national level. National consultations (like *Call to Action*) are, of course, always possible. Each nation and the episcopal conference must find its own way on the principle of subsidiarity.

SUMMARY

There are several advantages to the new approach of the revised canon law toward subsidiarity. The episcopal conference and plenary council can establish laws and policies at the local level. In this way, law can be adapted to local needs much more easily than under the former code. The episcopal conference has a responsibility to proceed with such legislation but with care and discernment. The code should not be seen as a complete recipe book for church order; the episcopal conference, therefore, should be judicious in legislating for the particular church and understand the need for subsidiarity on that level as well. The making of law on the regional level, however, also has the advantage of the ability to change law more rapidly than on the universal level. There is certainly a greater possibility for involvement of the ecclesiastical community in the formation of national policy and law both through formal intervention and certainly and above all through informal consultation.

There are some disadvantages to this process of law-making on the regional level. There is first of all the American danger of over-legislation. Americans seem to find it hard to leave matters to discretion and interpretation. It would be, in my opinion, very dangerous for the episcopal conference to begin legislating minute details that really should be left to provincial or diocesan law, just as it is dangerous for provincial or diocesan law to legislate matters that should be left to the discretion and interpretation of pastors. Secondly, we all recognize that the episcopal conference meets once or twice a year, and that it takes a long time for the episcopal conference to come to a decision. At times this may be viewed as a disadvantage, at times as an advantage and corrective to the American tendency to over-legislate. Finally, at the present time we have no clear way of promulgating and collecting regional law. The episcopal conference should develop a national church law digest or gazette where the decisions of the episcopal conference can be communicated in a clear and well-defined matter.

BERTRAM F. GRIFFIN, J.C.D.
Portland, Oregon

45

DIOCESAN CHURCH STRUCTURES

DIOCESAN SYNOD

Nine canons deal with the diocesan synod which is the legislative body on the diocesan level. True, the bishop remains the sole legislator in the diocese, but the synod is a powerful consultative body whose purpose is to assist the bishop in legislating the common pastoral good for the particular church. In the original draft, the synod was scheduled to be held at regular intervals, every ten or at most twenty years. At the last review this was removed, and the synod is now held at the discretion of the bishop in consultation with the presbyteral council.

The synod is composed of the auxiliary bishop and episcopal vicars, members of the presbyteral council, laity to be selected by the pastoral council, the urban and rural vicars, and one presbyter from each area or vicariate, the seminary rector, and religious superiors located in the diocese; even observers from the non-Catholic community may be invited.

The laws of the synod which have to be accepted and promulgated by the diocesan bishop, are to be forwarded to the metropolitan and the episcopal conference; they do not require the approval of the Holy See or even have to be sent there.

DIOCESAN CONSULTATIVE BODIES

Five consultative bodies are part of the post-conciliar Church. Two are obligatory: the presbyteral council (with the college of consultors), and the finance council (or administrative council). Two are optional though recommended: the diocesan pastoral council, and the episcopal council or bishop's cabinet. One is not mentioned in the revised code: the coordinating council of the apostolate, recommended by the Second Vatican Council (Decree on the Apostolate of the Laity, *Apostolicam actuositatem*, 26).

1. *The Presbyteral Council and College of Consultors*
The presbyteral council is required in every diocese. It is composed of the presbyters or priests of the diocese and is the "senate" of the bishop, representing the presbyterium. The statutes of the presbyteral council are approved by the bishop in accordance with the norms set up by the episcopal conference. The statutes should determine the membership of the council; approximately one half are to be elected by the presbyters themselves. Ex officio members are permitted as well as others named by the bishop as he so desires.

Those who have active and passive vote in the presbyteral council are all incardinated secular priests as well as secular externs and priests from religious institutes and societies who reside in the diocese and exercise an office for the good of the diocese. Particular law and statutes might also permit other resident priests such as members of religious orders without diocesan offices. The statutes should determine the manner of election; the diverse regions and ministries of the diocese should be represented.

The bishop convokes the council, presides over it, and sets a portion of the agenda by determining questions to be treated; members of the council can determine other agenda, but the bishop is free in receiving proposals for discussion and recommendation.

It seems that a five year term of office is presumed, although the actual term is to be determined in the statutes. When the see is vacant, the presbyteral council ceases and the college of consultors takes over. The bishop can dissolve the presbyteral council after consulting with the metropolitan, but he must reinstitute the council within a year.

The diocesan consultors are to be six to twelve priests appointed by the bishop from among the members of the presbyteral council. The consultors have a five year term, or if a consultor ceases as an elected member of the presbyteral council because of a shorter term of office he should be reappointed to the council as a bishop's appointee or serve as an ex officio member for the remainder of his term as consultor.

The college of consultors has two basic functions in the revised code.

First, the college acts as a governing board when the see is vacant. The presbyteral council ceases and the consultors remain. The new bishop submits his Apostolic Letters to the consultors and the chancellor. The consultors elect the administrator for the diocese who may not remove the chancellor or other notaries without the consent of the consultors. The college of consultors also acts as a governing body of last resort when the see is impeded (through captivity, exile, or inability of the bishop to communicate with his diocese). Finally, the coadjutor bishop must also submit his letters of appointment to the consultors and the chancellor.

Secondly, the college of consultors acts as a board of financial trustees of the diocese together with the finance council. The college of consultors must be consulted regarding the nomination and removal of the business manager, and both the college of consultors and the finance council must give their consent for extraordinary acts of administration and for the alienation of stable patrimony of the diocese within the limits set by the episcopal conference.

Although the presbyteral council is consultative only, the bishop is required to consult with the council of presbyters on several occasions, and the members of the council of presbyters (as mentioned above) have the right and obligation to participate in the diocesan synod and advise the bishop on legislation for the diocese.

The presbyteral council must be consulted whenever the bishop wants to erect, suppress, or make a notable change in parishes (c. 515). They must be consulted regarding the remuneration of priests who help in parishes when they are not pastor or associate pastor in that parish (c. 531). The bishop may establish pastoral councils in every parish after consulting the presbyteral council (c. 536). The bishop must consult the presbyteral council before imposing assessments on parishes (c. 1263).

2. *Personnel Boards*

Although personnel boards are not in the revised code, the concept of consultation is part and parcel of the new law. According to the new law, the council of presbyters and the bishop select a board of pastors which is somewhat equivalent to a combination of the former parish priest consultors and diocesan examiners in the 1917 Code. The bishop must consult at least two pastors from this board in the removal of impaired pastors (c. 1742) and in the transfer of pastors against their will to another parish or office (c. 1750). Moreover, the code instructs the bishop to consult the area vicar before appointing a pastor to a vacant parish within that vicariate (c. 524), and suggests that the bishop might well consult the presbyters and people. The bishop also is advised to consult the pastor and area vicar regarding the appointment of an associate pastor (c. 547).

Other elements of interest to personnel boards include the following:

The definition of an impaired pastor (c. 1741) includes behavior which causes grave harm or disturbance to the ecclesiastical communion: incompetence, lack of skill, mental or physical infirmity which prevent the pastor from fulfilling his role, loss of reputation or aversion on the part of serious and dedicated parishioners, serious neglect or violation of pastoral duties even after a warning, bad financial management (unless others means can be used to correct this problem), or any other behavior which causes the pastor's ministry to be harmful or inefficacious.

The episcopal conference can grant a decree permitting diocesan bishops to appoint a pastor for a definite term (c. 522).

Team pastorate is now in universal law. The pastoral care a parish or parishes can be entrusted *in solidum* to a team of priests. The entire team is pastor; one member is moderator who directs the common action and is accountable to the bishop (c. 517, §1).

The new universal law also permits lay exercise of pastoral care. Because of a lack of priests, the bishop can entrust a parish to a deacon, a lay person, or a lay and religious pastoral team, providing a priest acts as pastor and moderator (c. 517, §2).

Several neighboring parishes can be entrusted to one pastor because of lack of priests or for other reasons. Hence, there is not absolute need to reduce parishes to missions, to consolidate or close them merely because they lack a resident pastor (c. 526).

Pastors are requested to retire at the age of seventy five (c. 538, §3).

3. *Diocesan Finance Council*

The revised code requires every diocese to have a diocesan finance council, or a council on administration. The diocesan bishop or his delegate presides over this council which is composed of a least three members of the faithful (clergy or lay) qualified in financial matters and in civil law, and appointed by the bishop to a five-year renewable term of office. The finance council approves the annual financial statement of the diocese and prepares the annual budget in accord with the direction of the bishop.

The finance council must be consulted on several matters. The bishop, for example, may impose an assessment only after consulting with the presbyteral council and the finance council (c. 1263).

The bishop must consult the finance council for major administrative acts and must have its consent as well as the consent of the college of consultors for extraordinary acts as defined in universal law and the constitutional by-laws of the finance council (c. 1277).

The bishop consults the finance council in determining the extraordinary administrative acts of pastors (c. 1281).

Pastors and other administrators must make annual financial reports to the ordinary, who presents them to the finance council for the council's consideration; reports are also made to the faithful in keeping with the directives of particular law (c. 1287).

Bishops and pastors need the consent of the finance council and the college of consultors to alienate portions of the stable patrimony of the church in amounts determined by the episcopal conference (c. 1292).

The ordinary needs to consult the finance council prior to investing in trusts and foundations (c. 1305).

The ordinary needs to consult the finance council prior to reducing requirements of foundations (c. 1305).

4. *Consultation*

The fact the presbyteral council and the finance council are only consultative even though they are mandatory, should not discourage advocates of shared responsibility. Consultation in the revised code is not a mere pro forma act. Canon 127 states that if consultation is required by law, the majority of the group to be consulted must be consulted for the validity of the administrative act, unless particular law provides otherwise. If consent is required by law, it must be obtained for validity. Moreover, the administrator (bishop or pastor) should not act against the advice of consultors, especially if they are concordant, unless he has a prevailing reason. Hence, the code clearly recommends consensus management as a decision making style and process in the Church, allowing for discretion on the part of the bishop or pastor, but recommending that a consensus be achieved and that the administrator follow the consultation of appropriate bodies.

5. *Diocesan Pastoral Council*

The diocesan pastoral council is recommended both in the revised code and in the *Directory on the Pastoral Ministry of Bishops*. The pastoral council is basically a planning organization. It investigates, evaluates, and proposes practical conclusions regarding the pastoral activity in the diocese. It is composed of Catholics, members of the clergy, religious institutes, and especially lay persons representing various regions, social conditions, professions, and apostolates in the diocese. The pastoral council meets at stated times under the direction of the bishop and ceases when the see is vacant. It is consultative only and the bishop presides over the council and must convoke it at least once a year.

6. *Episcopal Council*

Another recommended agency on the diocesan level is the bishop's cabinet or episcopal council. The vicars general and episcopal vicars of the diocese form the episcopal council. One of the vicars general is appointed moderator of the chancery staff and his work is to coordinate the work of the curia and supervise the work of other staff members. All auxiliary bishops are also vicars general or vicars episcopal. The diocesan chancellor now is no longer required to be a priest. The chancellor in the 1917 Code as well as in the revised code is basically an office manager.

In the American Church, the office of chancellor, through delegation, became equivalent to a vicar general. Whether the American Church adopts the more traditional language and method of organization remains to be seen.

The episcopal vicars represent the bishop either in districts of the diocese, or with special groups such as language groups, or special ministries of the Church.

The code does not mention other offices such as superintendents of schools or Catholic charity directors. These two could obviously be included in the bishop's cabinet, if he so desires. The bishop's curia does have two support offices: the business manager who has a five-year contract, and the office manager or chancellor who may be a priest or a lay person.

7. *Coordinating Council for the Lay Apostolate*

The Second Vatican Council's Decree on the Apostolate of the Laity recommends that councils be set up on the diocesan and parish level to coordinate the various lay associations and undertakings, recognizing their particular nature and autonomy (*AA* 26). The coordinating council is not mentioned in the *Directory on the Pastoral Ministry of Bishops* or the Code of Canon Law, although both documents urge coordination of the lay apostolate on the diocesan, vicariate, and parish levels, by means of staff meetings, forums, and other group or intergroup relationships.

Canon 394 recommends that the bishop promote and coordinate the works of the apostolate, preserving their proper nature and autonomy. This coordination should be done on a diocesan or at least regional level. A council for this purpose is not included in the revised code.

Area vicars have as their first office, to promote and coordinate common pastoral action in the area (c. 555).

The absence of the coordinating council for the apostolate in the revised code does not mean that such a coordinating council is not a possible option for both the diocesan and parish level. As a matter of fact, on the parish level in this country, this particular passage from the Decree on the Apostolate of Laity (*AA* 26) is used as the Vatican II justification for the parish council. Unfortunately in many dioceses, the diocesan pastoral council is viewed as basically a coordinating council in the style of the paragraph of the Decree on the Apostolate of the Laity rather than as a planning council as described in *Christus Dominus* (*CD* 27).

OTHER STRUCTURES

It might be useful to point out other examples of Vatican II structures not mentioned in the revised code. Again let me add that their omission does not mean they are forbidden, but merely that they are now left to particular law and local option on the basis of the principle of subsidiarity.

1. *The Liturgical Commission*

This commission is mandated in the Constitution on the Sacred Liturgy (*SC* 45 and 46) along with a coordinated commission on sacred music and sacred art. The Instruction on the Proper Implementation of the Sacred Liturgy in 1964, and the Instruction on Music of 1967 repeat this norm. Interestingly enough, the *Directory on the Pastoral Ministry of Bishops*, like the revised Code of Canon Law, omits reference to liturgical commissions, sacred art commissions, or sacred music commissions.

51

2. *Catechetical Organization*

The *General Catechetical Directory* published by the Sacred Congregation for the Clergy discusses the organization for catechesis on the diocesan level and proposes structures whose purposes are to promote catechetical activities and to cooperate with other apostolic undertakings and works (for example, with the liturgy commission, associations for the lay apostolate, the ecumenical commission, etc.). The *Directory* does demand that every diocese have a catechetical office which is staffed and refers, on the parish level, to such structures as the parish catechetical center and the Confraternity of Christian Doctrine. The board of education, educational commission, etc., are not mentioned in the revised code.

3. *The Ecumenical Commission*

The *Directory Concerning Ecumenical Matters*, part 1, published in 1967, recommends a diocesan ecumenical commission. This commission is not mentioned in the revised code or in the *Directory on the Pastoral Ministry of Bishops*.

4. *Commission for New Parishes*

The *Directory on the Pastoral Ministry of Bishops* does suggest a diocesan commission for new parishes which works in consultation with the priests' council and other concerned commissions. This particular diocesan commission is not repeated in the revised code.

COORDINATION

The American Church since the Second Vatican Council has attempted to develop structures for shared responsibility. Unfortunately, we have often used political and business analogies. Hopefully the revised code will provide us with an opportunity to return to a more ecclesiologically founded form of church government. Our greatest temptation is to create hierarchical collegiality with extensive organizational charts showing how every organization, commission, apostolate in the diocese is coordinated by a super-board. The revised Code of Canon Law suggests the importance of coordination, but does not demand that this be done by a super-board or coordination council. The pastoral council is basically a planning council. Coordination might well occur through such agencies as the episcopal council or bishop's cabinet. In any event, the super-board which has delegates from all the other diocesan commissions has not demonstrated its effectiveness in the American Church on the diocesan level. The concept of such a super-board still persists, however, on the parish level, and perhaps needs to be challenged.

Political analogies are still being quoted in articles on church organization.

At one time, planners and amateur structural experts conceived of church government on the English model with the episcopal conference representing the House of Lords and the national pastoral council representing the House of Commons. The concept of a national pastoral council or parliament was considered not feasible several years ago. On the diocesan level, however, the presbyteral council is sometimes still viewed as a House of Lords and the pastoral council as the House of Commons—with the bishop as King George!

Some dioceses try to solve the problem of coordination on the French political model. The presbyteral council, the sisters' council, and a lay council organized with parallel authority are imagined analogously to the three Estates. Each of these councils sends delegates to a diocesan pastoral council viewed as an Estates General. The bishop alternates between the Sun King, trying to dissolve the pastoral council, and Louis XVI, being dissolved by it.

A friend of mine who studied in Rome suggests that the diocesan structure is really taken from Roman Law where the presbyteral council is the *Senatus* and the pastoral council is the *PopulusQue Romanus*. The bishop in this model comes out as Caesar or Imperator.

Another friend of mine who did not have the benefit of studying in Rome suggests that the bishop and his presbyters are basically analogous to King John and the Barons. The sections on rights and freedoms, and on due process in the revised Code of Canon law are the Magna Carta and the Second Vatican Council is Runnymeade.

The revised code, although adopting Montesquieu's division of powers into legislative, judicial, and administrative or executive, maintains nevertheless the tradition of the bishop as the sole legislator, sharing his legislative authority on a consultative basis with the diocesan synod and, to a lesser degree, with the presbyteral council. Diocesan financial administration is shared with the finance manager and the finance council. Judicial authority is exercised by the tribunal. The planning process occurs through the diocesan pastoral council and coordination of pastoral action is viewed on the diocesan level as a staff function of the episcopal vicars and, outside the chancery, as a coordinating function of the urban and rural vicars.

TRIBUNALS AND PASTORAL PLANNING

Without going into detail on the complex issue of procedural law, several elements of the revised code could be of interest to pastoral planners.

1. *Staffing*
The single judge permitted by the American Procedural Norms is retained in the new law with permission of the episcopal conference. The single judge must be a priest. The defender of the bond and the auditor may now be lay

53

persons. The procurator, the attorney, and the notary may be lay persons. The judge and the defender of the bond must have at least a licentiate in canon law.

2. *Appeal Process*

The appeal process must be conducted by a three-judge tribunal. At least one of the judges may be lay. An additional defender of the bond, who may also be lay, is required at the appeal level. All of these persons must have a licentiate in canon law. All cases must now be reviewed. The possibility of dispensation from review and appeal has been removed from the revised code, but the review can ratify an affirmative decision or admit it to a full hearing.

3. *Regional Tribunals*

Because of the additional personnel and the tremendous case load of local tribunals, I suspect that regional tribunals will be especially useful in the United States. These are now provided for in the new law under the episcopal conference.

4. *Privilege Cases*

The pauline privilege and the so-called petrine privilege are retained basically unaltered. Norms for privilege cases involving one baptized person are not given in the code but are governed by directives from the Congregation for the Doctrine of the Faith.

The effect of the revised code is going to demand the education of lay professionals and some financial outlay on the part of the Church. Hopefully, American ingenuity can provide word processors, computers, and other examples of technology to minimize the otherwise extravagant demand on both staff and money for vindicating and defending one's rights and freedoms.

THE PARISH

In the revised code the parish is defined as a stable community of the faithful within a particular church whose pastoral care is committed to a priest as the proper pastor under the authority of the diocesan bishop.

As a general rule, parishes are territorial. However, personal parishes may also be set up within a given territory with membership based on rite, language, national origin, etc. Hence, in the new law, multiple or cumulative membership in several parishes is even more possible than under the previous restricted notion of territoriality.

The pastor's ministry is a ministry of teaching, sanctifying, and governing or pastoring with the cooperation of other presbyters and deacons and in consultation with the laity.

The pastor has a finance council or council on administration; this is obligatory. The council itself has consultative vote and assists the pastor in the administration of the parish (cc. 537 and 532).

The diocesan bishop may establish a policy that every parish also have a pastoral council, and in doing so he must consult the presbyteral council. The pastoral council is to include the pastor, members of the parish staff, and members of the parish. The purpose is to promote pastoral action. The council has consultative vote (c. 536).

Coordination of parish organization and apostolates is not mentioned in the revised code nor does it mention how the finance council and the pastoral council relate. The American enthusiasm with hierarchical collegiality and super-boards has produced the "parish council," which performs all the functions of pastoral planning, administration, and coordination not only of the ministries of the parish, but often of all parish organizations and apostolates. This concept, of course, is not forbidden by the new law; but the law wisely suggests, in my opinion, that pastoral planning, administration and coordination of what we in this country call ministry (but which in the law is called the apostolate) might well be separate structural problems. With the introduction of the new law, the people in parish council ministry will, hopefully, have an opportunity to reflect on our past experience. It may well be that we will see emerging a true pastoral council on the parish level, leaving the development and coordination of ministerial committees and apostolic lay organizations to parish staff, thereby avoiding the growing sense of boredom on parish super councils where the only action month after month is hearing reports from committees, commissions and organizations, each having a reserved seat on the board.

BERTRAM F. GRIFFIN, J.C.D.
Portland, Oregon

PRESBYTERAL COUNCILS[1]

1.   Generally, the canons continue the law which has been in force since the Second Vatican Council when presbyteral councils were authorized.

2.   The purpose of the presbyteral council is clearly set for in canon 495:

   a.   It is a body of priests. Only priests are mentioned as belonging, no reference is made to include deacons.

   b.   It is to serve as the senate of the bishop. In the 1917 Code, this term is used for the cathedral chapter or, in this country, of the board of consultors. Clearly, the presbyteral council is to be the senate, the preeminent consultative body among priests.

   c.   The scope of the council's concern is quite broad—all those things which pertain to the pastoral welfare of the diocese.

   d.   The focus of the council's role is primarily in terms of governance. Governance in the revised code relates to the *"munus regendi"*—legislative, executive and judicial. While the council is consultative and not judicial or legislative, it has a concern for all those areas in a consultative manner.

3.   The council is to have its own statutes. It is not subject to whim or fancy, whether by individuals on the council or diocesan authorities. Once the statutes have been drawn up, taking into consideration the law and any norms which the N.C.C.B. may issue, they are to be approved by the bishop and then observed for the future.

Clearly, the revised code expects the statutes to specify a number of practical details. For example, canons in this section call for the statutes to deal with how many members are elected (about one half; the statutes can specify more), how many are ex officio; they can extend the right to vote and to run for office to priests living in the diocese who are not incardinated there or doing special service for the diocese; they determine how the elections are to run and the term of office for members.

The statutes may cover other matters as well. The constitutions of most senates already provide for a number of practical details and continue in force under the revised code.

4.   The revised code requires some adjustments in those dioceses where priests incardinated in the diocese may vote but, if they are outside the diocese, may not run for office. This, I think, is a minor detail and was recognized as such by the Code Commission. In the normal course of events,

[1]Editor's note: see also *United in Service: Reflections on Presbyteral Council*, approved by NCCB, November, 1991.

a priest who is outside the diocese would not be able to attend meetings unless special provision were made for this.

5. One of the changes introduced in the wording of the revised code relates to the bishop's relationship to the council. Canon 500, §1 may be interpreted as requiring a more direct involvement of the bishop in the ordinary operations of the council—calling meetings, setting agenda, chairing the sessions. I think this would be misreading the canonical tradition that underlies this canon.

The council is not to meet without the bishop's authorization; but the actual notifications of meeting, etc., do not have to be done by the bishop. Similarly, the sessions do not have to be chaired by the bishop; he can—and, for the sake of achieving the purpose of the council as a place of dialogue, reflection, and counsel, probably should—preside but let someone else chair the meeting itself. The same provision has been in effect relative to diocesan pastoral councils from the very beginning and the system of someone else chairing the meetings has proven feasible and profitable.

The circular letter of the Congregation for the Clergy on presbyteral councils (October 10, 1969) spoke about the bishop proposing items to the council or freely accepting issues raised by the members. The wording in the canons continues this position. This does not exclude other priests in the diocese from proposing items for the agenda; it does mean that the council retains control of its agenda, so that either a council member or the bishop himself would have to actually place the item on the agenda. It does not mean, however, that council members can deal only with items proposed by the bishop. Rather, the bishop is free to accept or not accept proposals the council has developed on its own initiative.

6. There are some cases in the revised code where the bishop must listen to the presbyteral council. These include whether to hold a diocesan synod; to set norms about stole fees, and about the support of those who do parochial ministry, whether full- or part-time. The bishop must consult the council on various pastoral matters: to erect, suppress, or make innovations in regard to parishes; to mandate parish councils in every parish; to give permission to build a church building or to permit an existing church building to be converted to profane use; to impose a diocesan assessment (other than the seminary tax).

7. The procedure for the removal of pastors has been revised. In the procedure the bishop must make use of two pastors drawn from a panel set up by the presbyteral council. That is, the bishop proposes a list of pastors to the council; the council selects those who will form an ongoing panel; when troubles arise, the bishop must draw on those approved by the council to form this panel, as part of the consultative process in removing a pastor.

8. The relationship of the presbyteral council to the college of consultors

has raised some problems in the past. The revised code attempts to resolve these in two ways. First, members of the college of consultors must be selected from among the members of the presbyteral council. As consultors they have their own term; but they may continue as members of the council. Indeed, there is nothing to prevent the statutes of the presbyteral council from keeping the members of the college of consultors on the council for the duration of their five-year term as consultors.

This approach has attempted to retain the freedom of the bishop to select advisors for certain key matters, but to continue the close tie of consultors with the preeminent clerical consultative body, the council. It may prove difficult in dioceses with very small councils, e.g., if the council has only fourteen members, the bishop will have to de-select two in order to meet the limitation of twelve members for the college of consultors. However, it is always possible to seek an indult to raise the limit within reason, and experience may point to other solutions to this problem.

The second way the revised code attempts to resolve the consultors-council issue is by limiting the issues the consultors may deal with. Canon 502, §1 indicates they are to deal with the matters specified in law. These include the naming and removing of the œconomus (finance officer) of the diocese, and certain other financial matters. Aside from those matters, the bishop is to consult with the presbyteral council (canon 495, §1) if he wishes to consult with a body of priests.

Moreover, there is nothing to keep the presbyteral council from dealing with financial matters, even though it is not bound to do so, and even though the college of consultors must deal with them. The bishop is not bound to seek the council's advice in these matters, but there is nothing which would seem to prohibit the council from offering its advice.

JAMES H. PROVOST, J.C.D.
Washington, D.C.

CONSULTATION WITH INDIVIDUALS OR GROUPS
REGARDING EPISCOPAL DISCRETION

Prenote: Canon 127, §2, 2° requires the bishop to consult in order to act validly in various diocesan undertakings. [Where *consent*, and not only consultation is required, will be indicated below.]

A. *Council of Priests* (cf. c. 500 on general rules re: consultative role)

   1. 461, §1: decision of bishop re: advisability of diocesan synod; no set time for synod.

   2. 515, §2: modification of parishes; i.e., erection, modification, division, suppression (cf. also c. 813 permitting bishop to set up university parish to meet pastoral needs of students; nothing explicit re: council of priests).

   3. 531: determination of use of offerings of faithful on occasion of parish services; to be placed in general parish fund.

   4. 536: decision re: appropriateness of parish councils and structuring of guidelines for such councils.

   5. 1251, §2: decision regarding permission to build a church (also to be consulted: rectors of neighboring churches).

   6. 1222, §2: decision to permit church to be converted to secular purposes for reasons other than its poor condition. (*Consent* of those with vested rights is also required.)

   7. 1263: decision regarding the imposition of diocesan tax for needs of diocese on public juridic persons subject to bishop; also, extraordinary and moderate tax for very grave needs to be imposed on other juridic persons and on physical persons (finance council also to be consulted). [New canon, not in 1917 Code, approved at October, 1981 Code Commission meeting.]

   8. 1742, §1: choice of stable corps of pastors from persons proposed by bishop to be available for processes of transfer or removal of pastors.

B. *College of Consultors* (c. 502: between 6 and 12 priests chosen by bishop from council of priests)

   1. 272: must consent before administrator can permit excardination, incardination or migration of clergy after see is vacant for one year.

   2. 485: consent for administrator to remove chancellor or other notaries.

   3. 494: hiring and firing of finance officer; finance council also to be consulted.

   4. 501, §2: *sede vacante* fulfills role of council of priests.

   5. 413, §2: choice of administrator in *sede impedita* situation if no other provision made.

   6. 419: governance of diocese initially *sede vacante* provided no other

arrangements made.

7. 421, §1: election of administrator with 8 days of vacancy.

8. 422: college to notify Holy See of vacancy.

9. 1277: bishop to obtain their consent for acts of extraordinary administration (along with consent of finance council).

10. 1292, §1: consent (with consent of finance council) to alienate diocesan property.

C. *Pastor-Consultors*

1. 1742, §1: preliminary discussion of possible removal of pastor with two pastors from group chosen by priests' council.

2. 1745, 2°: discussion of pastor's objections to removal with bishop.

3. 1750: discussion of pastor's objections to transfer with bishop.

D. *Dean*

1. 524: consultation re: appointment of pastor. (Other priests and laity *may* be consulted.)

2. 547: possible consultation re: appointment of parochial vicar [associate pastor]. (No explicit reference to consultation when parochial vicar is removed—cf. c. 552.) Pastor himself may be consulted re: appointment of parochial vicar.

E. *Finance Council*

Cf. c. 492, §1: a group of at least 3 experts in financial affairs and civil law, presided over by bishop or his delegate; laity or clergy without any distinctions. [Original schema provided for at least 1 member of priests' council to be a member of this group, but this was not retained as a requirement in the promulgated code.]

1. 493: to prepare annual budget according to bishop's determination and to submit annual financial report at end of fiscal year.

2. 494, §§1 & 2: hiring and firing of finance officer (along with college of consultors).

3. 494, §3: setting guidelines for functioning of finance officer.

4. 494, §4: finance officer to submit financial report to council. (537: no specific reference to finance council; but perhaps it should be consulted before bishop draws up guidelines for parish finance councils mandated in revised law.)

5. 423, §2: finance council to choose finance officer *sede vacante*, if finance officer elected diocesan administrator.

6. 1263: episcopal decision to impose taxes on physical or juridic persons (cf. no 7 under council of priests, above on "A" list).

7. 1277: bishop to hear finance council in significant administrative issues;

bishop needs their consent regarding acts of extraordinary administration (along with consent of college of consultors).

8. 1281, §2: episcopal determination of acts of extraordinary administration for institutes subject to his control if statutes do not specify this.

9. 1287, §1: examination of annual (financial) report of non-exempt administrators in the diocese.

10. 1292, §1: consent required for episcopal authorization of alienation within minimal and maximal sums determined by episcopal conference (also with consent of college of consultors, and of interested parties).

11. 1305: episcopal authorization to place money and mobile goods in a safe place and to invest them (interested parties also to be heard).

12. 1310, §2: episcopal reduction of burdens imposed in executing last wills for pious causes, if such burdens cannot be fulfilled (interested parties also to be heard).

Note: There is no explicit obligation for the bishop to consult the finance council in the following areas, but such consultation might well be in order. This is not to say that only the finance council need be consulted.

1. 1265, §1: permission of ordinary necessary for physical or juridic persons to collect money.

2. 1266: possible authorization of special collection to be taken up in all churches for various ecclesial undertakings.

3. 1274, §3: bishop to use common fund in diocese for various ecclesial needs.

4. 1276: ordinary to be vigilant re: administration of goods in public juridic persons subject to him; he is to issue appropriate guidelines.

5. 1281, §1: episcopal authorization of acts of extraordinary administration by subordinate administrators.

6. 1284, §2, 6°: episcopal consent necessary for investment of excess capital by subordinate administrators.

7. 1288: episcopal authorization for subordinate administrators to engage in civil litigation (cf. 1301-1302 for variance on execution of wills).

THOMAS J. GREEN, J.C.D.
Washington, D.C.

61

A BILLS OF RIGHTS AND FREEDOMS

In addition to the canons that specify the obligations and rights of clerics and religious, the code also includes obligations and rights of all the Christian faithful, ordained ministers and the laity:

1. The fundamental equality of all Christians based on baptism, and equality and dignity in action; the right and freedom to cooperate in building up the Body of Christ (c. 208).
2. The right to evangelize the nations (c. 211).
3. The right to petition, that is, to make known to pastors one's needs (especially spiritual) and one's hopes (c. 212, §2).
4. The right to recommend: the right to advise pastors regarding the good of the church, and to participate in public opinion and informing the faithful (c. 212, §3).
5. The right to receive the Word of God and the sacraments from pastors (c. 213).
6. The right to participate in worship in accordance with legitimate norms of one's own rite (c. 214).
7. The right to one's proper spirituality (c. 214).
8. The right to association: the right to found and direct associations with charitable purposes and as an expression of Christian vocation (c. 215).
9. The right to assembly: the right to hold meetings for the same purpose as to associate (c. 215).
10. The right to promote the apostolate and to one's own proper initiative in apostolic work, based on the right to participate in the Church's mission (c. 216).
11. The right to Christian education (c. 217).
12. Academic freedom: the right to research and to publication (c. 218).
13. Freedom from force in choosing one's station in life (c. 219).
14. The right to a good name and reputation (c. 220).
15. Privacy: the right to have others respect what is intimate to one's self (c. 220).
16. The right to vindicate one's rights in church court and to defend one's rights in church court (c. 221, §1) with equity and in accordance with law (c. 221, §2).
17. The right to be judged.
18. The right to legality regarding sanctions, that is, the right to expect the Church to impose sanctions only in accordance with law (c. 221, §3).

In addition, there are nine basic precepts listed in this same section of the code.

1. To maintain communion with the Church and fulfill one's Christian duties (c. 209).
2. To lead a holy life, and to promote the growth and holiness of the Church (c. 210).
3. To evangelize the nations, to announce the divine gift of salvation to all peoples, of every place and time (c. 211).
4. To obey church authority, both teaching authority and governmental authority (c. 212).
5. At times, to express one's opinion about what is for the good of the Church (c. 212, §3).
6. The obligation of parents to educate their children and to provide Christian education (c. 226, §2).
7. The obligation to promote social justice in keeping with the Church's teaching (c. 222, §2).
8. The obligation to care for the needs of the poor from one's own resources (c. 222, §2).
9. Finally, the ubiquitous precept to support the Church for the purposes of worship, the support of ministers and the works of the apostolate and charity (c. 222, §1).

The rights and freedoms are not stated as clearly and simply as in the above list. The Common Law tradition assumes that my rights and freedoms stop where your rights and freedoms begin. Hence, the Bill of Rights is a very simple and clear statement of the fundamental rights and freedoms. It is the business of the courts to establish the balance between rights and obligations. In the Roman Law and canonical traditional, it is the business of the legislator to spell out these restrictions, and the new code does so somewhat overgenerously.

Canon 223, §1 states that the exercise of rights is limited by considerations of the common good, the rights of others and obligation toward others. Canon 223, §2 states that, in view of the common good, church authority can regulate and moderate rights and restrict them by laws on invalidity or ineligibility.

Beyond these two restrictions, the rights and freedoms themselves are stated in a way that seems limited to someone coming from the Common Law tradition. Over and over again occur phrases like "according to one's proper condition and role . . . taking into account knowledge and competence . . . taking into account the integrity of faith and morals . . . taking into account

63

the common good . . . taking into account the dignity of persons . . . unless reserved, uniquely to Church authority . . . preserving due reverence for the magisterium . . . ," etc.

BERTRAM F. GRIFFIN, J.C.D.
Portland, Oregon

THE LAITY IN THE REVISED CODE

I. *Who are the laity?*

There are in the Church, by divine institution, sacred ministers, called clerics, and other Christian faithful, called lay persons (c. 204, §1).[1]

Lay persons are:

- configured to Christ by baptism
- strengthened in the faith by confirmation
- participate in the saving mission of the Church
- take on a specific work, especially that of giving witness to Christ in the ordering of temporal matters and secular affairs in accord with God (c. 225).

Lay persons are incorporated into Christ by baptism and, together with all the Christian faithful, constitute the people of God. Consonant with one's proper canonical state of life, each, in one's own way, participates in the priestly, prophetic, and kingly works of Christ. Thus, all the Christian faithful are called to exercise the mission which God entrusted His Church to fulfill in the world (c. 204).

II. *The revised code uses the term "Christian faithful". Who are they?*

The revised code directs itself to those of the Christian faithful who are in full communion with the Catholic Church on earth, viz.,

- the baptized joined with Christ in visible fellowship
- by the bonds of profession of faith, sacraments, ecclesiastical government (c. 205).[2]

These persons, incorporated into the Church of Christ by baptism, are at the same time constituted persons with all the duties and rights proper to a Christian (c. 96).

---

[1]From both of these groups, there are Christian faithful who by vow or other bond, recognized and ratified by the Church, profess the evangelical counsels and are consecrated in a special way to God (these persons are commonly known as "religious"—c. 207, §2).

[2]Catechumens, in a special way, are a part of the Christian faithful, joined with the Church and enjoying special prerogatives proper to Christians (c. 206).

Unless otherwise stated in the code those persons are not bound directly by merely ecclesiastical ordinances who have not yet accepted the Gospel and have not been baptized, and those baptized non-Catholic in Churches and communities separated from the Catholic Church, even though the former are related to the Church in various ways and the latter are joined in a certain, even if not perfect, communion with the Catholic Church (c. 11).

III. *What are these duties and rights proper to all the Christian faithful?*

All of the Christian faithful enjoy a true equality in dignity and action, and, according to one's proper state in life and work, are to cooperate in the building up of the body of Christ (c. 208).

All the Christian faithful:

- ought to lead a holy life, promoting the Church's growth and one's own sanctification (c. 210);
- have the duty and right to work together that the divine plan of salvation may touch more effectively all persons at all times everywhere (c. 211);
- are bound, conscious of one's own responsibility, to follow in obedience the teachings and rulings of the bishops (c. 212, §1);
- are free to make known to their pastors their wishes and needs, especially spiritual ones (c. 212, §2);
- have the right, and sometimes even the duty, according to one's knowledge, competence, and position, to make known to the bishops their opinions on things pertaining to the good of the Church, always showing concern for the integrity of faith and morals, and the common good and dignity of persons (c. 212, §3);
- have the right to worship God according to their own approved rite, and to follow their own form of spiritual life, consonant with Church teachings (c. 214);
- have the liberty to freely found and moderate associations for the purpose of charity or piety (when not reserved by their nature to Church authority) or for fostering the Christian vocation in the world; and to hold meetings for these purposes (cc. 215; 298-329);
- have the right to share in the Church's mission and to initiate on their own projects for promoting and sustaining apostolic activity (c. 215);
- have the right to a Christian education, the knowledge of the mystery of salvation, and instruction in right living, appropriate to one's maturation (cc. 217; 229);
- have the right to choose a state of life, free from all coercion (c. 219);
- have the right to a good reputation which no one may illegitimately harm (c. 220);
- have the right not to be punished by canonical penalties, except according to the norm of the law (c. 221, §3);
- have the right to vindicate and defend their rights in a competent ecclesiastical forum according to the norm of the law (c. 221, §1);
- have the right of appeal and the right to be judged by the prescriptions of the law applied with equity (c. 221, §2);
- have the duty to provide for the needs of the Church so that what is

needed for divine worship, apostolic works, charity, and a just sustenance for its ministers will be provided (c. 222);

- can exercise their rights individually or in associations, taking into account the common good of the Church, the rights of others, and one's duties toward others (cc. 222; 298-329).

Particular reference is made to:

- parents, who especially have the most serious duty and right to educate their children and to teach them according to the doctrine of the Church (c. 226, §2);
- students of the sacred sciences, who enjoy a freedom of inquiry, with due compliance to the magisterium of the Church; indeed, they should prudently declare themselves in those matters in which they are competent (c. 218).

A final canon in this section in the code notes that the ecclesiastical authority is competent to moderate for the common good of all the above rights or to restrict them by invalidating or incapacitating laws (c. 223, §2).

IV. *Are there specific duties and rights proper to the lay Christian faithful?*

Lay persons have the duty and right, individually or in associations, to work that the divine message of salvation may be made known and accepted by all persons everywhere in the world. This duty is all the more urgent in situations where people can hear the Gospel and know Christ only through lay persons (c. 225, §2).

Lay persons are to be acknowledged as possessing the right to civil liberty; however, in exercising that right, they should take care that their actions are imbued with the spirit of the Gospel and that they direct their attention to the magisterial teaching of the Church, sincerely avoiding proposing their own opinions as Church teaching in debatable matters (c. 227).

Lay persons who are married have, by reason of matrimony and the family, a vocation and an office to work for the building up of the people of God. Moreover, they have a right to pastoral and canonical assistance in this area from the pastors of the Church (c. 226, §1).

Lay persons who qualify can be called by bishops to ecclesiastical offices and works, in accord with the law, and those who are outstanding in due knowledge, prudence, and honesty, can assist bishops as experts and counselors (even in synods, councils, etc.) in accord with the law (c. 228).

Lay persons have the duty and the right to acquire a knowledge of Christian teaching so that in exercising their part in the apostolate they may live it, proclaim it, and, if necessary, defend it. Therefore, they have the right to attend ecclesiastical universities and schools of religious studies and to receive academic degrees. Those who qualify, in accord with the law, can receive the mission to teach the sacred sciences from legitimate ecclesiastical authority (c.

299).

Lay men who qualify can be instituted permanently to the ministries of lector and acolyte (however, this does not confer on them the right to sustenance or remuneration from the Church) (c. 230, §1).

All lay persons can be deputized temporarily to serve in the office of lector, and all enjoy the faculty of serving in the offices of commentator, cantor, and others, according to the norm of the law (c. 230, §2).

Lay persons, in cases of need when there are no sacred ministers, can supply for these offices by ministering the Word, presiding at liturgical prayer, conferring baptism and distributing Communion (c. 230, §3).

Lay persons who permanently or temporarily give themselves to a special service of the Church are obliged to be properly formed for this work, and they have a right to a fitting and proportionate remuneration to provide for themselves and their families, and, to the extent that it can be provided, social security and health insurance (c. 231).

V. *How does all of this actually affect the lay person?*
The revised code offers:
- a more detailed and extensive treatment of the duties and rights of the lay person (cc. 204-205; 207; 224-231);
- less discrimination; all the baptized constitute the people of God, and, while there are obviously diverse offices and duties, all are equal in dignity and common action by reason of baptism (cc. 204-205; 207-208);
- a special emphasis on the common priesthood of the faithful with the lay person participating more actively in the Eucharist and offering his or her priestly ministry in sacramental actions, prayer, thanksgiving, charity, and witness of a holy life (cc. 204-205; 208; 210-216; 225; 327-329);
- more extensive involvement on the part of the lay person, including the holding of an ecclesiastical office and cooperating in the exercise of the power of governance (cc. 124-145), e.g., as a judge in a collegiate tribunal (c. 1421, §2);
- more consultative involvement, e.g., as delegates at diocesan synods (cc. 460-468), members of the diocesan pastoral council or a parish council[3] (cc. 511-514; 536), parish leadership roles and on-going pastoral leadership positions for ongoing pastoral care (c. 517).[4]

---

[3]These are not mandatory institutes but are to be instituted if pastoral solicitude recommends it.

[4]A priest directs these activities since only a priest can be a pastor of a parish (c. 521, §1).

Lay persons now can:

- exercise an increased number of non-ordained ministries, where needed, e.g.,
    - chancellor (c. 483)
    - notary (c. 483)
    - procurator-advocate (c. 1483)
    - promoter of justice (c. 1435)
    - defender of the bond (c. 1435)
    - judge (c. 1421, §2)
    - diocesan business managers (c. 494)
    - members of diocesan or parish finance councils (cc. 492-494; 537)
    - represent the person of the Holy See as members of Pontifical Missions or as members of heads of delegations to international councils, conferences or congresses (c. 301)
    - acolytes[5]
    - lectors[6] (c. 230; 910, §2)
    - extraordinary ministers of the Eucharist
    - deputized extraordinary ministers of exposition of the Blessed Sacrament (c. 943)
- preach[7] (c. 766)
- receive the canonical mission to teach theology and other sacred sciences (c. 229, §3)
- be missionaries (c. 784)
- be catechists (c. 785)
- be assigned to act as extraordinary ministers of baptism (c. 861, §2)
- be delegated to assist at weddings (c. 1112)[8]
- administer Sacramentals (c. 1122).

The revised code stresses the role of family and its vocation in building up the Church (c. 226, §1). Parents are the primary educators of their children and have freedom of choice in the selection of schools (c. 793). All others are to assist them in this goal of education.

The revised code emphasizes the parish as a community of persons (cc. 515-552). Lay persons are called to a more active role (cc. 517, §1; 528). As cited

---

[5]Only males may be acolytes (c. 230, §1).

[6]Only males may be permanent lectors (c. 230, §1). Other lay persons can be deputized temporarily to serve in the office of lector (c. 230, §2).

[7]The homily at the Eucharist, however, is reserved to priests and deacons (c. 767, §1).

[8]The bishop may do this with the authorization of the episcopal conference and the Holy See (c. 1112, §1).

above, they can participate in a wider variety of offices and ministries, some formerly reserved to clerics.

In addition to the contents of these canons, lay persons continue to possess a strong moral power, a strong innovative influence. They continue to maintain the power of receiving or not receiving all of the law or some of the law. Ultimately they still possess the power of numbers, of finances, of public opinion, of *sensus fidelium*, of conscience and the radical power of shaking the dust from their feet as they exit or worse, stay on apathetically.

RICHARD C. CUNNINGHAM, J.C.D.
Brighton, Massachusetts

JURISDICTION FOR LAITY[1]

Canon 517, §2 provides the canonical basis for the growing phenomenon worldwide and even in the United States of placing non-ordained ministers in charge of parishes. The canon provides:

1. This arrangement may be made only in situations where there is a shortage of priests. The situation is "extraordinary" even though it may be the usual experience of the people as in some mission areas or a prolonged situation as is foreseen in parts of the United States and Canada.
2. The judgment as to the advisability and conditions for implementing this canon is left to the diocesan bishop.
3. The bishop has three options under this canon:
    a. He may appoint an ordained minister (deacon).
    b. He may appoint an non-ordained minister (who is of course qualified for the position and is granted the necessary deputation and faculties).
    c. He may appoint a team of lay ministers.

Language for this position is still fluid in the United States, although there are indications that the preferred title is parish minister (for the deacon or lay minister) and parish ministry team (for the team mentioned in the canon).

4. Note that it is the diocesan bishop who entrusts the parish to a parish minister. The appointment could not be made by other local ordinaries without special mandate.
5. The parish minister "participates in the exercise of pastoral care." Full pastoral care, of course, can only be exercised by a priest. It would be advisable for the bishop to define the rights and duties of the parish minister and the limits and extent of their participation in the exercise of pastoral care, either by particular law or in the letter of appointment.
6. The bishop is also to appoint a priest to moderate or supervise the pastoral care. This priest is also known by several titles in the United States, but language seems to be standardizing on the title "(parish) priest moderator."
7. The priest moderator is not technically a *parochus*, but he is to be endowed by the bishop with the powers and faculties of a parish priest. Diocesan legislation, or at least the letter of appointment, should define

[1]From: *Roman Replies and CLSA Advisory Opinions* 1987, William A. Schumacher and J. James Cuneo, eds. (Washington, D.C.: Canon Law Society of America, 1987) 91-100.

and grant the necessary powers and faculties and hopefully clarify the relationship between the priest moderator and parish minister(s).

The priest moderator ordinarily cares for several parishes in a cluster or pastoral zone. Participation in the exercise of pastoral care in these parishes is conducted by lay people, deacons, or pastoral teams. The parishes remain open and active even though the diocese lacks sufficient priests to appoint a resident parish priest for each. The priest moderator provides supervision and that pastoral care reserved to priests or specified in the letter of appointment.

Can the non-ordained parish minister with such an appointment exercise any parochial jurisdiction?

In the strict sense a *parochus* or parish priest has only minimal power of jurisdiction or *potestas regiminis* by reason of his office.

The parish priest does not have the legislative, judicial, or executive power of a local ordinary (cc. 129 & 135). However, canon 519 refers to his exercise of the *munus regendi* or governing role which includes:

a. Certain habitual faculties granted by law or the diocesan bishop (c. 132).
b. The *potestas dispensandi*—an extension of executive power and, therefore, the power of jurisdiction (cc. 85 and 137-142). Ordinarily, the parish priest may not dispense unless this power has been expressly granted him. The code and diocesan faculties grant such powers in several cases.
c. Pastoral authority or commissions. Several pastoral functions are committed to the authority of the parish priest (c. 530). This authority may be called "jurisdiction" in a wide sense.

The parish priest moderator is also endowed by law and the diocesan bishop with faculties.

I. Habitual Faculties
The parish priest and priest moderator possess several faculties.

A. Confirmation (cc. 882-883).
In danger of death, the parish priest, the priest moderator, and any presbyter may confirm. The parish priest in this country by mandate baptizes adults and receives already baptized adults into full communion. Hence by office the parish priest and priest moderator may also be granted additional faculties to confirm by the diocesan bishop.

Clearly neither the ordained (deacon) nor non-ordained parish minister may share in these faculties.

B. Penance.

The parish priest and priest moderator possess the faculty to hear confessions within their jurisdiction by virtue of their office (c. 968, §1). Again, neither the ordained deacon nor the non-ordained parish minister may share in these faculties.

C. Marriage.

The parish priest and priest moderator by virtue of their office are the canonical witnesses at marriage (c. 1108) and can delegate this faculty to other priests and to deacons within their territory (c. 1111). Ordinarily, the lay parish minister does not share in this faculty.

Canon 144 supplies jurisdiction in cases of common error or positive and probable doubt in the above three faculties.

Marriage: A Special Case.

However, in virtue of canon 1112, a non-ordained parish minister could be granted the faculty to assist at marriages by the diocesan bishop. Since the bishop could grant him or her habitual faculties, this seems to be a case where a non-ordained person "cooperates in the exercise of jurisdiction" at least in the wide sense (c. 129, §2).

Note ten juridic steps in providing for a lay minister to witness marriages in the name of the Church.

1. Enabling legislation. Under the 1917 Code, neither deacons nor lay persons could be granted the faculty or delegation to witness marriage. The 1983 Code has enabling legislation for deacons in canons 1108, §1 and 1111, §1 and for lay persons in canon 1112.

2. Prior favorable opinion of the conference of bishops. The Canadian bishops have voted to obtain this indult. In November 1989, the National Conference of Catholic Bishops (U.S.A.) recommended "to the Holy See that it favorably entertain the request of those individual diocesan bishops who, in view of the severe shortage of ordained ministers in certain vast territories of the United States, seek the faculty to delegate lay persons to assist at marriages"[2]

3. Permission of the Holy See. The Canadian Conference of Catholic Bishops and the N.C.C.B. have obtained such permission.

4. Decision of the diocesan bishop. Implementation is up to the diocesan

---

[2]*Implementation of the 1983 Code of Canon Law. National Conference of Catholic Bishops: Complementary Norms* (Washington, D.C.: United States Catholic Conference, 1991) 15.

bishop.

5. Qualification or certification of the lay minister. Canon 1112, §2 states that the lay minister,
    a. must be suitable;
    b. must be capable of providing pre-marriage formation;
    c. must be qualified to celebrate the marriage liturgy correctly.

Hence, the diocese would need to initiate a training program and standards for certification.

6. Authorization. Even after a person is qualified as suitable, it is the diocesan bishop who designates a lay person as an official minister of the Catholic Church authorized to witness marriages in the name of the Church.

7. Registration. In some states (as in Oregon) the authorized minister (whether ordained or not) must register with the county before civil law permits him or her to witness marriages. A letter of authorization from the chancery is presented to the county clerk.

8. Appointment. In many dioceses even priests and deacons, though authorized by their ordination to perform marriages, are not given general faculties to do so unless they are appointed to a pastoral office (parish priest, parochial vicar, a deacon appointed to a parish as parish minister or to a parish staff as an associate, a university chaplain, etc.). It would seem appropriate to limit the use of lay ministers as official ministers of marriage to those appointed as parish ministers or some similar pastoral office.

9. Delegation. The diocesan bishop grants the delegation (either in single cases or habitually) to the lay parish minister, to be exercised in the absence of the priest moderator. General faculties would presumably be given in the letter of appointment.

Note that the priest moderator does not have the power to delegate the lay minister even if he or she has been authorized as an official witness. The priest moderator may delegate another authorized priest or a deacon (c. 1111, §1); only the diocesan bishop may delegate the non-ordained parish minister.

10. Permission. Since marriage is a function committed to the parish priest (or priest moderator), the parish minister needs at least the presumed permission of the priest moderator for a particular marriage (c. 530, §4).

If the parish minister has general faculties from the diocesan bishop, may they be sub-delegated? Since habitual faculties are governed by the prescription for delegated power (c. 132, §1), it seems logical that the parish minister could sub-delegate a priest or deacon for a particular marriage. (In a real life scenario, the priest moderator is absent on vacation and has granted permission to the parish minister with habitual faculties from the bishop to witness a marriage next Saturday. The parish minister falls ill and delegates a permanent deacon visiting in the parish for that marriage.) Since the diocesan bishop but not the pastor delegates a lay person to witness marriage, it would seem illogical for the lay parish minister to be able to sub-delegate another lay minister for this marriage.

D. Preaching.

All priests and deacons have the faculty to preach everywhere (c. 764). This faculty is a form of teaching jurisdiction. The faculty, like delegated jurisdiction, may be restricted or removed by the competent ordinary. Prior to the present code, dioceses granted faculties to preach to visiting clergy. Pastors could delegate this faculty according to diocesan norms. The faculty to preach was considered the jurisdiction to preach. Now the presumption is in favor of the faculty granted by law. By reason of canon 766, lay persons can be granted the faculty to preach if it is necessary, or even useful, in particular cases. The lay parish minister who leads the Sunday assembly on those days when the priest moderator is celebrating the Eucharist in another parish would likely have the faculty to preach in the diocese from the diocesan bishop. This habitual faculty is a form of jurisdiction or a "cooperation in the exercise of the power of jurisdiction." It should be noted that granting a lay person the faculty to preach does not relieve the parish priest or priest moderator from his obligation to preach a homily when he celebrates the Mass. Lay persons may preach sermons but not the Eucharistic homily (c. 766).

II. The Power to Dispense

The law grants the parish priest (and, therefore, also the priest moderator) the power to dispense in several circumstances. This power to dispense is an extension of the *potestas regiminis* and is, therefore, a form of jurisdiction.

A. The parish priest (and priest moderator) may dispense their own subjects as well as travelers from private vows (c. 1196, §1) and from promissory oaths (c. 1203). This power is not granted the parish minister by law.

B. The parish priest and priest moderator can in individual cases dispense from the obligation to observe a feast day or day of penance or can commute the obligation to other pious works (c. 1245). This power is not granted the parish minister by law.

C. As confessors, the parish priest and priest moderator can remit in the internal sacramental forum any undeclared *latae sententiae* excommunication or interdict (c. 1357, §1) when recourse to the competent superior would be hard on the penitent; and in danger of death, any censure can be remitted (c. 976). Such power to remit is analogous to the power to dispense; obviously the lay parish minister cannot exercise this power.

D. The confessor and the priest or deacon with faculties to witness marriage can grant certain dispensations in the area of marriage law. Obviously these powers to dispense apply to the parish priest or priest moderator.

1. In danger of death, the parish priest or priest moderator and the properly delegated sacred minister (priest or deacon) can dispense from the canonical form and all impediments of ecclesiastical law except the impediment arising from the sacred order of priesthood when the local ordinary cannot be reached.

2. In danger of death, the confessor can dispense from occult impediments for the internal forum.

3. When wedding preparations are made and there is danger of delay, the above persons can also dispense from occult impediments of ecclesiastical law except the impediment of sacred order or public perpetual vow of chastity in a religious institute of pontifical right.

Since the lay minister delegated to witness marriage is not mentioned in these canons, he or she lacks such power to dispense even in danger of death or when all preparations for the wedding have been made and there would be danger in delay. This may be a *lacuna* in the law which Rome could remedy by indult for those countries where the episcopal conference has been granted permission to delegate lay persons as official witnesses.

III. Special functions committed to the authority of the parish priest and priest moderator (c. 530)

This pastoral authority is an exercise of the *munus regendi* of the parish priest and is only jurisdiction in the wide sense. The authority is possessed by the parish priest or priest moderator. In some cases the lay parish minister may exercise these functions with at least the presumed permission of the priest moderator. The lay minister does not exercise jurisdiction in these areas of law but performs the functions under the "jurisdiction" of the pastor.

1. The parish minister may be deputed to baptize by the local ordinary (c. 861, §2). He does so under the authority or "jurisdiction" of the priest moderator.

2. The parish minister, deputed as an extraordinary minister of communion, may administer Viaticum with permission of the priest moderator.

3. As stated above, the parish minister with faculties to witness marriages from the diocesan bishop, may do so with permission of the priest moderator.

4. The parish minister with permission of the moderator may celebrate funerals, but obviously not the funeral Mass.

Some committed functions may only be exercised by the priest moderator and not the lay parish minister.

1. Confirmation in danger of death.

2. Anointing of the sick.
3. Blessing of the baptismal font during the Easter season and the imparting of a solemn blessing outside the church (the code does not grant lay people to power to bless: c. 1169).
4. Celebration of the Eucharist on Sundays and holy days. Only a priest may celebrate the Eucharist of course. The parish priest has special responsibility for the Eucharist on Sundays and holy days. The lay parish minister may be deputed to preside over the Liturgy of the Word on Sundays in the absence of the priest moderator and may minister Holy Communion. The lay minister may also preside over a Communion service during the week.

Summary

The parish priest does not exercise the jurisdiction of a local ordinary. Jurisdiction is the power of governance and includes legislative, judicial, and executive power. The parish priest governs the local Church or parish under the authority of the bishop with pastoral authority and shares in some jurisdiction both by reason of office and by diocesan faculties. The parish priest in consultation with the pastoral council enacts pastoral policies but does not have legislative authority. The parish priest is often involved in conflict resolution but does not have judicial power. The parish priest supervises pastoral care and has pastoral authority in certain areas committed to him but he does not have the executive authority of a local ordinary. However, the parish priest in this country has the mandate to baptize adults and to receive already baptized adults into full communion of the Church. He, therefore, has by law and by reason of his office the faculty to confirm them as well as to confirm those in danger of death. By reason of office, he has the faculty to celebrate the sacrament of reconciliation and to delegate other priests and deacons to assist at marriages in his territory. By reason of his ordination he has the faculty to preach.

The parish priest also has the power to dispense in areas granted him by law. The power to dispense is an extension of executive power and is hence jurisdiction.

Finally, the parish priest governs the parish under the authority of the bishop and certain pastoral functions are committed to his authority. The law states that the priest moderator is endowed with the power and faculties of the parish priest and commentators add as well the authority to supervise pastoral functions which are especially committed to the parish priest.

The lay parish minister may cooperate in the exercise of jurisdiction according to the norm of law. He or she may be admitted to preach, thus sharing in this form of jurisdiction. In some countries the lay parish minister may be delegated by the bishop to assist at marriages with permission of the priest moderator, thus receiving faculty to perform marriages and marriage jurisdiction. The law does not grant to the lay minister the power to dispense in any case.

Finally, the lay minister may be deputed to perform certain pastoral functions under the authority or "jurisdiction" of the parish priest. The bishop may depute the lay minister to baptize, to act as extraordinary minister of Communion and even Viaticum, to preside over the Liturgy of the Word and distribute Communion at the Sunday assembly (and during the week)—all under the authority and supervision of the priest moderator.

The 1983 Code, therefore, provides three examples where lay people cooperate in the exercise of the power of jurisdiction.

1. They may cooperate in the judicial jurisdiction of the Church as a lay judge on a tribunal with two other clerics (c. 1421, §2).
2. They cooperate with the pastoral jurisdiction of the Church by:
   a. being admitted to preach when necessary or even when useful in particular cases. When the priest moderator is present for Mass, however, he is obliged to preach the homily. The lay person may preach a sermon but not the Eucharistic homily.
   b. by receiving the faculty to witness marriages under the supervision of the priest moderator and with his permission if the Holy See, the episcopal conference, and the diocesan bishop so decide. Lay people who have this faculty, however, may not grant dispensations in the area of marriage, at least according to the law.

A Final question

Many dioceses grant the parish priest and priest moderator (and indeed many other priests and deacons) additional faculties and powers to dispense. In the Portland Archdiocese the parish priest and priest moderator, for example, have the power to dispense from the impediment of disparity of cult under the usual conditions. Moreover, they are authorized to celebrate mixed marriages and several of the pastorally sensitive marriages listed in canon 1071 without the need to obtain permission from the bishop. May the diocesan bishop grant similar faculties to the non-ordained parish minister? May the bishop grant to the lay parish minister the power to dispense in other areas which the law attributes to the parish priest?

A conservative reading of the law implies that the bishop may not do so. Canon 129, §2 states that lay members of the Christian faithful can cooperate in the exercise of the power of jurisdiction "in accord with the norm of law." Canon 89 states that the parish priest and other presbyters or deacons cannot dispense from a universal or particular law unless this power has been expressly granted to them; no mention is made of granting this power to lay members of the Christian faithful. The norm of law grants to lay persons the ability to "cooperate in the power of jurisdiction" only in the three areas mentioned above.

A more liberal reading of the law would permit the local ordinary to delegate dispensing power and the granting of permissions to lay persons (e.g., a lay chancellor or lay parish minister). According to this opinion, the law does not grant dispensing power, but the ordinary may grant delegation to dispense. The issue is disputed by canonists; the Apostolic Delegate in a private letter recognizes the *dubium iuris* and recommends that such delegation not be granted as the safer course.

BERTRAM F. GRIFFIN, J.C.D.
Portland, Oregon

PERSONNEL ISSUES

I. INTRODUCTION

In recent years we have witnessed a dramatic increase in the number of lay persons becoming involved in formal church ministry. Various theories have been proposed to explain this phenomenon. Those of more traditional background suggest the serious shortage of vocations to the priesthood and religious life as the reasons why more lay people must become involved. Others of a different pastoral perspective suggest that the phenomenon stems not so much from the shortage of vocations as from a renewed emphasis on the basic baptismal call to Christian service. The discussion has resulted in a debate about who are qualified for Christian ministry and who for Christian service. The discussion is not over, but the new code clearly recognizes the need for lay persons to participate in the exercise of pastoral ministry in collaboration with a presbyteral or episcopal moderator or overseer. It would seem the intent of the code is to maintain a basic connection between the power of orders and the power of jurisdiction. Therefore, the exercise of formal lay ministry and, to a great extent, the ministry of the deacon, is ordered to those activities which do not require those powers intimately connected with priestly ordination. In practice, deacons and lay persons may certainly be considered collaborators in ministry and even carry out significant pastoral responsibilities in partnership with members of the presbyterate.

As with that section of the code which deals with the rights and obligations of the clergy, commentators and practitioners should bear in mind that the new code reflects the doctrine and documentation of the Second Vatican Council, in effect moving the Church from Vatican I to Vatican II. Pastoral practice since the close of Vatican II, coupled with the reflections of theologians, may legitimately influence the interpretation and application of the code to personnel issues.

Most, if not all, personnel offices are still directed toward the distribution of clergy personnel, including in many dioceses, permanent deacons. Some personnel offices have begun to function as clearing houses for lay persons seeking a pastoral position within a parish or other pastoral institution. However, the appointment of non-clerical persons is not a canonical appointment nor does it carry with it any official canonical title, e.g., pastor, associate pastor. Some diocese have accepted a title such as "parish minister" or "pastoral associate." Although commissioning ceremonies have been designed to solemnize the appointment of parish ministers to pastoral staffs, such ceremonies are not assumed to have canonical force. Nevertheless, the justice and the basic rights of Church members must be recognized and safeguarded in the employment practices and policies governing lay ministry.

Latest reports indicated that the number of priests can be expected to decline over the next two decades. It will become increasingly necessary to promote lay ministry and new pastoral structures through which the Church will be able to continue her mission. The code has at least opened the door toward a more creative approach to pastoral ministry. Several dioceses are already well on the way toward a more holistic approach to collaborative pastoral ministry without dishonoring the norms prescribed in the new code.

II. SELECTED PERSONNEL ISSUES

A. *The Appointment of Pastors and Associate Pastors*

1. Only a priest can be validly appointed pastor (cc. 521, §1; 517, §1; 150). His appointment should be based on those qualities and virtues necessary for the responsible exercise of his office (cc. 521; 547).

2. The diocesan bishop is the one who freely appoints pastors and associate pastors (cc. 521; 547).

3. In appointing a pastor, the bishop has the obligation of assigning the priest whom he considers suitable in view of all circumstances. Therefore, the bishop is not required to appoint the one subjectively most qualified.

4. In determining the suitability of a candidate, the bishop should seek the advice of the vicar forane, who may conduct an appropriate inquiry. The bishop may also consult other priests and even lay persons (c. 524).

It is under this canon that the role of the personnel director and the personnel board should be discussed. It is clear from the code that the personnel director and the board are advisory to the bishop, who retains full freedom. However, the bishop may not act arbitrarily nor should he show favoritism. It should be kept in mind that although it is the responsibility of the vicar forane to be solicitous for the welfare of the priests within his vicariate, he must also look to the common good of all the people. The vicar forane is not a vicar for clergy. It must be assumed that the needs of a parish are to be seriously considered in determining the priest most qualified to be appointed pastor.

5. Ordinarily, a pastor should be appointed as the pastor of one parish (c. 526, §1). Moreover, in the same parish there can be only one pastor. In the case of a shortage of priests, one pastor may be appointed pastor of several neighboring parishes. It is important to note that these neighboring parishes retain their identity as parish. They are not reduced to the status of a mission. Moreover, the code serves to envision the collaboration of lay persons with the pastor.

This canon excludes the appointment of co-pastors to one parish. However, two priests may be appointed to form a team *in solidum*. In this case, one of the team must be appointed "moderator" (c. 517, §1).

6. Term of Appointment. The new code stresses the stability of the office of pastor. His appointment, therefore, is for an indeterminate period of time (c. 522). All indults to the contrary cease with the promulgation of the code (c. 6, 2°). Episcopal conferences may issue a special decree permitting the bishop to limit the tenure of pastors. The episcopal conference must first seek the confirmation of such a decree from the Holy See in the usual manner (cc. 522; 455, §2).

No mention is made of tenure for parochial vicars (associate pastors). The new code does state that the bishop may remove or transfer an associate pastor "for a just reason" based on the needs of another parish or on those of the parish to which he is assigned.

Other than the right he has as a member of the Christian faithful and as a cleric, the code does not seem to provide for any specific rights for associate pastors other than a period of one month vacation. However, the bishop may approved diocesan policies which honor the human need for security and stability with due process in the assignment process. The whole trend of recent documents on the relationship of bishops and priests emphasizes the mutuality of this relationship. The code envisions the whole presbyterate as primary collaborators in the government of the diocese. Parochial vicars are to pastors what episcopal vicars are to the bishop of the diocese. Therefore, associates are primarily collaborators with the pastor.

7. Removal of Pastors

a. No one appointed to an office which he holds for an indefinite period of time can be removed except for serious reasons and only by following the procedure described in the law. The same applies for a priest assigned to an office for a specified period in order for him to be removed before termination of that period (c. 193).

Conditions which justify the removal of a pastor include behavior which may cause serious harm to the pastoral community; mental invalidity or permanent physical illness which renders the pastor incapable of carrying out his duties; loss of reputation in the eyes of serious-minded parishioners or hostility toward the pastor which is unlikely to dissipate; serious neglect of pastoral responsibilities which persist in spite of warning; inefficient administration of temporal goods resulting in serious harm to the Church without possibility of resolution (c. 1741).

b. Procedure for Removal (cc. 1740-1747)

1) When the bishop has reason to believe there is sufficient case for removal, he must confer with two pastors selected from among those approved for this purpose by the presbyteral council.

2) If after consultation with the two pastors the bishop feels that the serious reasons require the removal of the pastor, he will prudently

ask the pastor to resign within fifteen days.

3) If after two requests the pastor does not submit his resignation or refuses to do so without giving reasons, the bishop is to issue a decree of removal.

4) If the pastor decides to contest the bishop's action, he is permitted to examine to records of the case and respond in writing. After examining the pastor's written response and, if necessary, after a hearing, the bishop is to discuss the matter with the same two pastors. After this deliberation, the bishop is to decide whether to remove him or not.

5) Once the decree of removal has been issued, the pastor must vacate the parish. If the pastor is ill, the bishop should allow him to remain on the premises for as long as necessary.

6) The pastor still has recourse to the Holy See against the bishop's decision.

7) During this appeal, the bishop may not appoint another pastor but may appoint an administrator.

Comment: The process for the removal of a pastor is administrative, not judicial. Although a last-resort measure, it is not intended to be punitive. Although the consultation with the two pastors is required, the bishop is not bound to follow their counsel, though he would be imprudent to disregard it without serious reason. The bishop must still provide for the sustenance of the pastor by giving him another assignment or by directly providing an adequate income.

8. Transfer of Pastors

a. Transfer looks more to the good of the parish to which the pastor is to be transferred rather that the welfare of the parish from which he is being transferred. The code offers two reasons to justify a transfer: (1) the good of souls and (2) the necessity or utility of the Church. In fact, any worthwhile reason would justify refusal on the part of the pastor (c. 190, §2).

b. Procedure for Transfer (cc. 1748-1752)

1) Bishop proposes the transfer in writing.

2) If the pastor refuses, he should give his reasons in writing.

3) If the bishop's decision remains firm, he should follow the same procedure as that outlined for the removal of a pastor.

9. Retirement. A pastor is urged but not absolutely obliged to submit his resignation upon the completion of his 75th year. The bishop will then decide whether to accept or defer the resignation (c. 538, §3). Retirement policies adopted by several dioceses in the United States will need to be re-evaluated in light of this new legislation. If a bishop wishes to impose retirement on an unwilling pastor, he must follow the procedure for the removal of a pastor. It may also be opportune to review the use of the term "retirement."

Although a priest may retire from an office, he does not really retire from priesthood. Much more discussion is needed in this area.

10. Residence. Pastors and associates are obliged to reside in a parish house near the church. The bishop can permit residence elsewhere provided they can still carry out their parochial functions adequately (c. 533, §1). The code strongly recommends communal residence for priests (c. 550, §1).

B. *Team Ministry*

The code recognizes a new entity called "team ministry" (c. 517, §1).

1. When circumstances require it, the pastoral care of one parish or even of several parishes simultaneously can be entrusted to several priest acting as a team, *in solidum*.

2. One of the priests on the team is to be appointed "moderator" of pastoral care with the responsibility of coordinating joint activities of the team and be accountable for the team to the bishop (c. 517, §1).

The moderator is an episcopal appointment.

The code makes no mention of anyone except priests as members of the team. The code, however, does recognize other "parish ministers" or "pastoral associates" as collaborators with priest members. In practice they certainly may collaborate in the exercise of pastoral ministry in those areas for which priestly ordination is not required. Parish ministers or pastoral associates are not to considered canonical appointments. They may be considered members of the pastoral staff.

3. More than one parish can be entrusted at the same time to the same ministry group (c. 526, §1).

4. Team members and the moderator enjoy permanent stability and, therefore, are appointed for an indefinite period (c. 542, 2°; cf. c. 522). Therefore, all members of the team share the same responsibilities as pastors.

5. Removal or transfer of the moderator or team members must honor the requirements for removal or transfer of pastors (c. 544; cf. cc. 1740-1752).

6. In legal action, only the moderator acts in the name of the parish or parishes entrusted to the team (c. 543, §2, 3°).

7. If one of the priest members or the moderator withdraws or if one of them becomes incapable of exercising the pastoral ministry, it does not result in the vacancy of the parish or parishes (c. 544). The bishop shall appoint another moderator should he withdraw, etc. Until the appointment of a new moderator, the senior priest assumes the role of moderator.

8. All team members are bound by the obligation of residence (cc. 543, §2, 1°; 533, §1; 550, §1).

KENNETH E. LASCH, J.C.D.
Paterson, New Jersey

CANONICAL STANDARDS IN LABOR-MANAGEMENT RELATIONS[1]

Current church law is based on the official teaching of the Church's magisterium and is expressed in the 1983 Code of Canon Law. The new code also draws on the Church's centuries-old canonical tradition. These sources contain substantive provisions which bear directly on the sensitive issue of labor-management relations in church institutions, agencies, and offices.

Within a Roman Catholic context, the relationship between employers and employees is a moral question. This relationship has been the topic of formal attention by the Church's magisterium, including the teaching of all the popes in this century, the college of bishops at an ecumenical council, and bishops teaching in their own dioceses or gathered as a conference of bishops. The magisterium's teaching in this case is on a question of morals, and Catholics are conscious they must approach the issues involved in this relationship from this moral perspective, prior to financial, legal, and other considerations.

However, questions of labor and management are not exhausted by examining their moral dimensions; there are also legal questions in both civil and canon law. The Church as an institution and individual Catholic institutions, agencies, and programs are required to work within the framework of church law, as well as other sources, when searching for solutions. The purpose of this paper is to examine briefly those sections of church law which have a bearing on the field of employer-employee relationships in order to extract general standards within a context from which more specific practices and procedures can be developed. Only when the legal issues are clearly differentiated from the economic constraints and the interpersonal relationships of any particular situation, will there be a possibility for morally acceptable, just, and reasonable resolutions of difficult labor-management situations in the Church.

Implementation of general standards may vary somewhat from state to state, as the law of the several states varies; it may also vary with the type and conditions of employment, as the diversity and complexity of the employment situation vary. Yet in all implementation, the law and teaching of the Church remain normative.

Grounding for a just policy in the labor-management field can be found in four general areas of the Church's law:

1. Law governing the employer-employee relationship;
2. Law on associations;

---

[1]For a complete report on this topic see *Canonical Standards in Labor-Management Relations: A Report* in CLSA *Proceedings* 49 (1987) 311-335.

3. Law on contracts;
4. Law on other fundamental rights.

These general areas can be summarized by twenty statements:

1. Out of the employer-employee relationship there arises both rights and duties for all parties involved. In the Church these rights and duties are not isolated claims and responsibilities, but are to be integrated in the overall communion of the life of the people of God.
2. Provision is to be made for a just and equitable compensation so that workers may adequately provide for themselves, their families, and others who depend on them. Wages and benefits must be at least be up to the standards set in the applicable civil laws.
3. Working conditions are to be assured which respect the dignity of the persons involved and must at least be up to the standards set in the applicable civil laws.
4. The Church's teaching and law on employer-employee relationships apply to direct and indirect employers, including subcontractors.
5. The local ordinary, and in particular the diocesan bishop, has a vigilance role over all church related activity in the diocese, including the observance of church law on employer-employee relationships.
6. The dignity of the human person within the common good is the yardstick by which all considerations regarding the relationships between employers and employees are to be judged.
7. Church administrators are bound to observe the standard of diligence of a good householder. In enforcing this norm, the diocesan bishop can determine more precisely what this standard entails, and in doing so may take into consideration even those civil laws from which the Church is exempt.
8. All persons have the natural right to assemble freely and to form associations for legitimate purposes. Church teaching recognizes that these purposes include those of collective bargaining and other activities proper to labor unions.
9. The Church's law recognizes the fundamental rights to assemble and to form associations, and affirms them within the Church itself.
10. Associations for collective bargaining or labor unions have been proposed by the Church as appropriate means for persons to exercise similar rights in secular society, and in the Church.
11. No types of work, no areas or segments of the workplace, are excluded *a priori* from the formation of labor unions or associations for collective bargaining, including diocesan offices and church related institutions, agencies, and programs.
12. Associations formed by the Christian faithful, while they are under the vigilance of church authorities, are governed by the members them-

selves in keeping with their statutes.

13. The presumption is that civil laws in the United States are generally in conformity with church teaching; the diocesan bishop is the competent authority to decide if a specific civil law is not to be observed because it is contrary to church teaching or to canon law.

14. These fundamental rights apply within the Church as well as in secular society; *a fortiori*, they apply to church related institutions, agencies, and programs which employ persons in carrying out their activities.

15. In keeping with fundamental equality in human dignity, there is to be no discrimination on the basis of race, color, sex, national origin, handicap, or age in employment by church agencies or institutions. Affirmative action is an appropriate means to overcome existing discrimination.

16. Persons have a right to participate in coming to decisions which affect their lives.

17. They have a right to express their needs, and to participate in the formation of public opinion about matters in which they enjoy some competence or experience.

18. They have the right to enjoy their good reputation, and not to have it damaged unlawfully.

19. They have the right to privacy and to access to some files which concern their status as a person.

20. They have the right to vindicate their rights, and to the resolution of disputes in the Church.

THE PASTOR'S ROLE
AND SOME IMPLICATIONS FOR SEMINARIANS

I. MINISTRY OF THE WORD

The first obligation of the pastor is the ministry of the Word, (passing on our tradition). The pastor does this principally.
1. by preaching a homily every Sunday and on holy days of obligation;
2. by his responsibility for catechetic instruction in the parish;
3. by encouraging programs which promote the Gospel spirit, especially regarding social justice.

The pastor has a special responsibility for the Catholic education of the children and young people in his parish.

With the help of other members of the congregation, the pastor is responsible for evangelization of those who have not yet heard the Good News or of the unchurched and those who are no longer active in the Church (c. 528, §1).

It is the proper duty of presbyters, who are cooperators with the bishops, to announce the Good News. Pastors and others who have the care of souls are particularly responsible for announcing the Good News to their congregation or communities (c. 757).

Although presbyters and deacons (unless their faculty is restricted by the local ordinary or unless particular law requires permission) have the faculty from universal law to preach everywhere, the pastor presides over the pulpit, and the presbyters and deacons must at least have his presumed permission before they preach in the parish church (c. 764).

The pastor presides over the pulpit and over preaching in the parish church. He is to preach, or to see that a sermon is preach on every Sunday and on holy days of obligation. He may not omit the homily without serious reason. It is recommended that homilies also be preached at daily Mass, particularly during Advent and Lent, or on the occasion of a funeral or a special celebration (c. 767).

The pastor should also arrange for other forms of preaching, spiritual exercises, missions, and retreats (c. 770).

The pastor is responsible for the members of his congregation who rarely, if ever, are able to hear the Word of God. He should see that they receive appropriate instruction. He is also responsible for evangelization of the non-believers in his parish (c. 771, §1).

The pastor has a particularly serious obligation and responsibility for the catechetical instruction of his people (c. 773).

By reason of his office, the pastor is responsible for the catechetical formation of adults, young people, and children in his parish. In exercising this responsibility he should enlist the aid of other clerics, religious, and members of the laity, especially catechists (c. 776).

It is the special responsibility of the pastor to oversee
1. general sacramental catechesis;
2. the preparation of children for first Communion and first reception of the sacrament of reconciliation;
3. for the Sunday School and the extension of catechetical instruction of children who have already made their first Communion;
4. for catechetical instruction of the handicapped;
5. for the catechetical instruction of adults, both apologetics and enrichment of the Christian life (c. 777).

Since the pastor is responsible for evangelization, canons which refer to the obligations of missionaries are also applicable to the pastor. For example, in evangelization the pastor should make use of catechists, that is, lay members of the congregation or the diocese who are educated and trained for this role and who, under the pastor's moderation, direct the catechumenate (c. 785).

Implications

If preaching, catechetics, and evangelization are the principal responsibilities of the pastor, then the diocese has a right to expect that seminarians complete their course of studies with a firm grasp of Scripture and of tradition, and an understanding of the principles and methods by which the tradition is passed on in homiletics, catechetics, and evangelization. We do not expect seminarians to be research scholars, although some may be asked to go on for further studies. All seminarians, however, should be well trained in Scripture, systematic theology, moral theology, the social teaching of the Church, church history and church structures, and be competent to pass on the Gospel and our tradition in the pulpit, the classroom, and the pastor's study.

II. LITURGICAL LEADERSHIP

The second basic responsibility of the pastor is liturgical presidency.

It is the pastor's responsibility to see that the liturgy in his parish is celebrated in accordance with church norms, and that the active participation of the laity in the liturgy is promoted. The pastor should see that the Eucharist is the center of the congregational life of the parish. It is his responsibility to see that the faithful are devout in their reception of the Eucharist and the sacrament of reconciliation. The pastor promotes a spirit of prayer in the parish and in the families of the parish (c. 528).

Pastors are responsible for seeing that the faithful are sufficiently evangelized and catechized before reception of the sacraments (c. 843, §2).

Initiation. The pastor presides over the sacraments of initiation; celebration of the sacrament of baptism is reserved for the pastor or those to whom he delegates his office. It is the pastor who is responsible for administration of confirmation in danger of death, and it is the pastor who presides over the blessing of the baptismal font.

Although the deacon and other presbyters are also ordinary ministers of baptism, and when the deacon or presbyter is absent or impeded, a catechist or another specially delegated lay person can celebrate the sacrament of baptism, nevertheless, it is the pastor who presides over the sacraments (c. 862).

Hence, it is also the pastor who will confirm catechumens after their reception of the sacrament of baptism (cc. 883; 866).

It is the pastor's responsibility to see that children who have attained the use of reason are immediately catechized and prepared for the sacrament of first Communion, (c. 914).

Sunday Eucharist. It is the pastor who presides over the Eucharist on Sundays and holy days of obligation or at least over the principal liturgical celebrations of those days (c. 530, 7°).

Sacrament of Reconciliation. The pastor is responsible for celebrating the sacrament of reconciliation for the faithful and providing opportunities for individual confession on specific days and at specific hours (c. 986).

Marriage. The pastor presides over the celebration of marriage in his parish (cc. 530, 4°; 1063; 1109).

1. through preaching, appropriate catechesis of young people and adults, the use of mass media, all of which can instruct the faithful regarding the meaning of Christian marriage and the duties of Christian spouses and parents;

2. personal preparation for entering marriage by which the spouses are prepared for the sanctity and obligations of their new state in life;

3. by a true liturgical celebration of marriage in which it is clear that the spouses represent and participate in the mystery of unity and creative love between Christ and the Church;

4. by assistance to married people and through family life ministry for married couples (c. 1063).

Summary and Implications

1. Just as the bishop presides over the liturgy for the particular church, so the pastor presides over and celebrates the Eucharistic liturgy for the local parish church with the assistance of other liturgical ministers, either temporary or permanent—lectors, acolytes, cantors, extraordinary ministers of the Eucharist, ushers, psalmists, commentators, choirs, etc.

2. And, as the bishop presides over the *Pax*, or the sacrament of reconciliation, for the particular church and entrusts a share of this ministry to the presbyters of his diocese, so in a special way the pastor is responsible for providing opportunities for reception of this sacrament, both in communal celebrations and at stated times during the week.

3. Just as the bishop presides over initiation for the particular church, so the pastor presides over initiation for the local parish church. Deacons and catechists may baptize. It is the pastor who confirms the baptism of those received into the Church after the use of reason. The deacon or catechist might baptize infants, but only under the moderation and supervision of the pastor. The pastor confirms in danger of death. The present law only reserves the confirmation of children baptized Catholics as infants to the bishop. The baptism of young people over the age of fourteen should be referred to the bishop but in this country such baptisms are usually celebrated on the local level under the direction of the pastor.

4. Finally, the pastor presides over the sacrament of marriage with the assistance of catechists and deacons.

Hence, the seminarian should have a firm grasp of sacramental theology and discipline and above all, a clear personal liturgical piety centered on the Eucharist. Unlike religious, who might spend the majority of their life con-celebrating, hearing confessions in retreat settings, and never celebrating the sacraments of marriage or initiation, the diocesan priest, being trained for the pastorate, should have a clear understanding of the role of the sacraments in a pastoral setting and be prepared to exercise liturgical pastoral leadership in this area.

III. PASTORAL MINISTRY

The office of pastor includes the responsibility of knowing one's parishioners.

1. Parish visitation is important and puts the pastor in touch with the concerns, the problems, the griefs and the joys of his people, participating with them, comforting them, and intervening as a guide and a counselor when appropriate.
2. The pastor has a special care for the sick, especially those close to death, helping them with his counseling and his prayers and the sacraments.
3. The pastor has a special responsibility for the poor, the afflicted, the lonely, the immigrant, the exile, and those with special problems.
4. The pastor has a special responsibility for family ministry, supporting spouses and parents in their duties and way of life (c. 529, §1).

Implication

Hence, the seminarian must be introduced to such pastoral skills and activities as:

1. Pastoral Conversations—whether in the privacy of the church office, in a restaurant over lunch, in the family living room, at someone's bedside in a hospital room, at the place of work. Personal counseling, particularly on issues of religious and personal importance, is one of any pastor's major activities.
2. Pastoral Convening—it is the pastor's initiative which leads him to bring people together in various groups for various purposes, acting as a reconciler, as a group leader, initiating dialogue, playing the role of mediator or arbiter, or merely enabling encounters.
3. The pastor is present in the great creative events of life: childbirth, coming of age, choosing a vocation, marriage. The pastor has to have a sense of celebration of these moments and of the Church's concern for these highly teachable events in people's lives, and the pastor needs skills for dealing with crisis situations where people are suffering, distressed.
4. The pastor is going to need a certain amount of knowledge and technique in the specific area of pastoral counseling.

IV. ENABLING MINISTRY

The pastor should promote the appropriate mission of the laity in the Church and support various lay associations for religious purposes. Moreover, it is up to the pastor to develop a sense of the laity's participation in the mission of the particular church of the diocese and of the works and mission of the universal Church (c. 529, §2).

Pastors should be expected to develop among the laity a sense of shared responsibility and planning for the pastoral action and mission of the parish through parish councils (c. 536).

Throughout the code there are several references to the development of lay mission and ministry, particularly in the area of catechetics and liturgical ministries.

Implications

Hence, the seminarians should be trained to have a sense of, and the necessary skills to develop shared responsibility, both in government and in ministry on the parish level. The pastor is involved intimately in the lives of his parishioners. This, however, does not mean that the pastor hugs ministry and decision-making to himself, but, precisely *because* of his intimate involvement in the lives of so many people, he must enable them to take responsibility for the mission and direction of the Church through the many ministries of the local church, both regarding the Church's outreach mission to the world and the Church's ministry to its own members.

V. ADMINISTRATION

Finally, the pastor is the legal representative of the parish and is responsible for the administration of church property and finances (c. 532).

The pastor will be assisted by a finance council or committee made up of lay members of the congregation (c. 537).

Implications

Parish administration was not taught in the seminary prior to Vatican II; priests learned parish administration by oral tradition from their fellow pastors. Certainly parish administration must be taught by the diocese in the new pastor classes which every diocese should begin to initiate. Nevertheless, it does seem that seminaries could give some broad principles and understandings of parish administration, both financial and in terms of personnel management. More and more pastors are going to have to understand job descriptions, charters of accountability, personnel policies, grievance procedures, contracts, as well as balance sheets, budgets, taxes, insurance, security, fund-raising, etc. Admittedly, much of this will be done by lay volunteers, but in very small parishes the pastor cannot avoid certain direct administrative responsibilities. In very large parishes, the pastor must have an over-all understanding of parish administration even if he has a staff person with the direct responsibilities for administration itself.

SUMMARY

Hence, the pastor and, therefore, the seminarian preparing for the ministry of pastoring should be trained and skilled in five areas:
1. the area of preaching and teaching, his primary task;
2. the area of liturgical celebration, particularly the Eucharist, in a pastoral setting, his co-primary task;
3. the area of pastoral care, or counseling;
4. the area of Church leadership and enabling shared responsibility in ministry;
5. the area of Church administration.

BERTRAM F. GRIFFIN, J.C.D.
Portland, Oregon

CANON LAW AND PARISH MINISTRY

Let us focus, for a moment, on the familiar and the unfamiliar; the known and unknown.

All of us have a parish, we know our parishes and, in all likelihood, participate not only in the life of the parish but also serve in some kind of leadership position in the parish. The parish is familiar; the known; the place where most Catholics come in contact with their Church. What does a parish mean? It is the place where we first experience the educational and sacramental mission of the Church. The parish is our neighborhood link with other Catholics, the place where we experience community and express our values. Because the parish is so familiar, we tend to take our own experiences and expectations and transfer them to other parishes. Sometimes we even take the parish for granted, take its ministers for granted and attempt to continue that memory of past parishes into the present one. What may not be so well known, so familiar, is canon law, Catholic church law, and what it says about the parish, what it expects of the parish, how it expresses the dream for the parish. To bring these two ideas—the parish and canon law—together we are going to look at **the parish, its mission, and its ministers.**

As a canon lawyer, I would like to warn you about one of my prejudices—I think canon law is a gift to the Church. It's not, of course, always the gift we would pick out for ourselves, its not even the perfect gift, but canon law is that body of principles, exhortations, expectations, and rules that summarize for us who we are as Catholics, what makes us Catholic, what we have learned from the past, how we relate to one another and the key elements of Catholic ministry. The material in canon law is organized under seven headings, called books. It is obvious that the canons cover most aspects of the Church's public life:

I.   General norms give us the basic definitions and principles of application;

II.   The people of God describes who we are;

III./IV. The teaching and sanctifying mission define and organize essential actions in the community;

V.   Temporal goods gives meaning, direction and accountability for those material things that are necessary for the Church's mission;

VI.   Sanctions defines the limits of the community's tolerance of insult and offense;

VII.   Procedures provide the basic rules of community decision making and the fairness we have the right to expect when we deal with others.

That law is, though, a human creation—and humans and their words are limited. As a result, the gift—the values, strengths, and usefulness—of canon law is not always immediately evident. The law has no value unless it comes to life in the community, is applied and interpreted, and becomes a part of the way we think about ourselves. Everything you wanted to know about being Catholic is **not** in the Code of Canon Law—it expects faith, discipleship, charity, and even hope. But what the law does do is provide the basic shape of how we live as Catholics. It is based on the clearly articulated principles (in the list of obligations and rights of all Christians) of the dignity of each and every one of us and the bond of communion we share (cc. 208; 209). Our canon law, revised in the light of the insights of the II Vatican Council, says some important and challenging things about **parishes, its mission, and its ministers.** To see what it says, we can look to three canons: 515; 528; and 529.

The canons are found in the second book called the People of God. Notice that the canons first of all describe the Christian faithful and then the constitution of the universal Church with the pope as its pastor, the diocesan Church with the bishop as its pastor. The **parish,** along with the diocesan synod, the diocesan offices and consultative bodies, is a part of the internal ordering of the particular church, the diocese.

Canon 515—the first canon in the section on parishes—is new in our law. It gives the basic description of a parish—a kind of definition—by identifying four essentials:

> The parish is a **definite community**
> established on a **stable basis**
> by the **diocesan bishop**
> entrusted to a **pastor** as its own shepherd.

Notice how the canon begins: a parish is a definite community of the Christian faithful. The community must be definite, that is, be defined, have limits, be clearly identified. Notice that the canon does **not** say that a parish is established on a territorial basis. That is clarified in another canon (518) where territory is established as the general rule, but any stable community can be established as a parish. We know of some from the past—those parishes that were established for special language or nationality groups for example—but the new canon gives much broader discretionary authority to the diocesan bishop when it says that any determining factor can be a reason for establishing a parish—as long as that factor is stable. That provides great flexibility for the diocesan church in meeting the needs of the Christian faithful. What other stable communities exist in your dioceses? Are there particular needs that could be best met by designating a definite community

95

as a parish?

The choice of the word "community" was a deliberate one on the part of those who drafted the canon. On one hand, the parish is **not** described as a "church" (not the building, of course) because the parish is a part of a particular, local, diocesan church. That is based on our ecclesiology—what we say the church is—which identifies the college of bishops and its head as an essential constitutive element in the Church. In order for a group to be a "church", in our tradition, a legitimately ordained and appointed bishop must be the head. On the other hand, the parish **is** described as a community to suggest that special bond of familiarity which is to be characteristic of a parish. What does that fundamental concept of the parish as community suggest? The canons don't spell it out, but the bond is always to be one of faith and hope and love. It suggests a place where we share the same values and live them out as individuals and in a community. It suggests diversity and co-responsibility. It is a rich new concept that needs our continual prayer, reflection, and discussion. What does it mean to say the parish **is** (not should be, or can be, or ought to be) a community?

The parish, secondly, is established on a **stable** basis. That is, members of the community can expect that their parish will be there for some time. A parish, in other words, is not established on a temporary basis. Stability is a significant aspect of the trust we should be able to have in the community and is enshrined in canon law in many places. One of the functions of law in the community is to protect us all from arbitrary and capricious behavior, or, more positively, to guarantee regular, fair, and dependable expectations of how the members of the community will act. Because the parish is such an important and immediate contact with the Church, the law attempts to ensure stability of the community, its ministers, and its mission.

Because the parish is a part of the diocesan church, canon law requires that the diocesan bishop, and only the diocesan bishop, establish parishes. Law (and canon lawyers) likes to be able to trace clear lines of responsibility and authority so the canons identify the diocesan bishop as the legal authority. The bishop's role, of course, is more important than that which the law gives him. In fact, that is putting the cart before the horse. In other words, the bishop does not have authority in the particular church because canon law gives him that authority. It is rather that canon law identifies that authority because of the role of the diocesan bishop as the Pastor of the particular church.

Finally, the important canon 515 requires that each parish be entrusted to a **pastor** as its own shepherd under the authority of the bishop. The office of pastor, given minimal shape in canon law, evokes images of the past, the joys and frustrations of the present, images of tyrants and friends, saints and scholars, and of Bing Crosby and Barry Fitzgerald (probably the most famous pastor of all!). The pastor is related to both the bishop and the community in a special relationship of responsibility. Quite clearly, canon law wants to establish who is responsible—both to the bishop and the community—for the parish but, beyond that, the concept of pastor and its long history provides a fruitful area for reflection for both pastors and communities.

The pastor is not only responsible for the parish programs, buildings, and finances, he is also responsible for coordinating and enabling the members of the parish to live out their Christian responsibilities. Apart from the fact that the pastor must be a priest and must be appointed by the bishop, the canons provide a new flexibility and realism in describing the office of pastor. One individual or several can be responsible alone or together for one or several different parishes. In addition, the new canon 517, §2 provides for the possibility of participation in the exercise of pastoral care in a parish by those who are not priests.

The canons, then, provide for a new description but very little shape for the parish. That community which is a parish, however, does not just exist for itself—to provide a cozy refuge in a threatening world. The parish has a **mission**.

The parish mission, of course, is intimately related to the mission of the world-wide Church and the diocese. All Christians share in the priestly, prophetic, and sanctifying mission which Jesus has entrusted to the Church in the world. That mission is challenging and rewarding, general and specific, shares in what is ancient and what is new, is frightening and consoling at the same time. Is there a specifically "parish mission"? Something about what members of the parish do that makes its mission unique?

I think there is. That uniqueness is closely related to the code's definition of the parish as a community—a place where people know and care about one another, not in the abstract, but personally and intimately. There are two canons that speak of the parish mission and suggest how all of us participate in it.

A basic agenda for the parish:

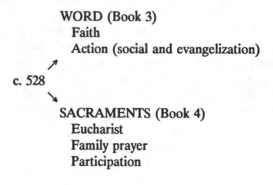

WORD (Book 3)
Faith
Action (social and evangelization)

c. 528

SACRAMENTS (Book 4)
Eucharist
Family prayer
Participation

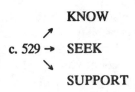

KNOW

c. 529 → SEEK

SUPPORT

The **mission** of the parish, indeed the mission of the entire Christian community, only takes place because people actively participate in it.

In that important sense we are all **ministers**—each and every member of the parish community, according to talents, interest, insights, and ability, with dedication, enthusiasm, humility, and prayer is called upon to serve others. A friend of mine used to have one instruction that summarized the attitude that should characterize the Christian community—think of others **first**. Within the community of the parish, fortunately, we have a variety of gifts and a multiplicity of talents. Within the parish community we have varieties of service and degrees of responsibility. The Code of Canon Law recognizes, organizes and directs that variety of ministers—the ministry of the pastor which is so clear in law and practice, the ministry of parents living out the conjugal life and raising their children, the ministry of deacons, religious, catechists, extraordinary ministers of the Eucharist, lectors, those who visit the sick, feed the hungry, and give shelter to the homeless. Wisely recognizing that it is impossible for a document written for the whole world to address every nation and community, the code leaves the shape of those ministries and ministers to the wisdom of local churches. It expects the diocesan bishop to recognize needs and initiative, to facilitate dialogue and planning, and to authorize those ministries which are, in his judgment, best for his local church. As ministers participate more and more "officially" in the mission of the Church, the code provides some helpful directions for fairness in employment and contracts, appointment, evaluation, and support. Should it be necessary, the code provides a model for dismissal, for rebuke, and expects open and honest procedures to protect rights—both of individuals and the local church.

But all that takes us too far afield . . . because the basic insight of the code is the unity of the Christian community—a unity in belief, in discipline, and in mission. The expectation of the code is that the parish community, by the way it lives its mission in a particular time and place, will make the Church ever more present. That, finally, is the only purpose of canon law in the Church. It helps us to keep in touch with our roots, to relish our tradition, to respond to contemporary needs, and to serve one another with respect and gentleness.

That law is very limited; it is an aid, an instrument, a help which enables us to appreciate that "in Christ Jesus the life giving law of the Spirit has set us free from the law of sin and death" (*Rom.* 8:2). It is that Spirit that animates a parish, brings fruitfulness to its mission, and enlivens its ministers.

EDWARD G. PFNAUSCH
Washington, D.C.

PARISHES WITHOUT A RESIDENT PASTOR:
COMMENTS ON CANON 517, §2[1]

Canon 517, §2 states a new canonical possibility, one which is very likely to be implemented in many local churches, but it does not provide lengthy details about its canonical or practical implementations. Nor are the canon's provisions referred to elsewhere in the code. Canon 517, §2 states:

> If the diocesan bishop should decide that due to a dearth of priests a participation in the exercise of the pastoral care of a parish is to be entrusted to a deacon or to some other person who is not a priest or to a community of persons, he is to appoint some priest endowed with the powers and faculties of a pastor to moderate the pastoral care.

Questions:

We know that a number of dioceses, in order to offer needed pastoral services to the faithful, have implemented the provisions of this canon. Frequently, a number of questions arise in that implementation. Very few authors have commented upon the canon, and no authentic interpretation has been offered by the Pontifical Commission. I wish in the remainder of this article to raise some questions about the implementation of the canon, to offer some indications of answers if possible, and then to provide some concrete suggestions which may be of service in implementing the canon. I will term the priest mentioned in canon 517, §2 the "priest-moderator." The deacon, lay person, or community of persons, will called, in the singular, the "parish coordinator." I believe these to be accurate and acceptable designations.

1. When may the provision of canon 517, §2 be implemented?
It is clear from the history of the development of the canon that required for its implementation is a shortage of available clergy. It is the responsibility of the diocesan bishop, in overseeing the many needs of the diocese for clergy, to determine when the time is ripe to implement the canon. It may be prudent for him to involve the diocesan pastoral council and the presbyteral council in assessing the placement of priests and the appropriateness of present structures. He may also wisely seek the counsel of the local dean (see

---

[1]From: "The Canonical Implications of Canons 517, §2: Parishes without Resident Pastors," John A. Renken in CLSA *Proceedings* 50 (1988) 249-263.

cc. 524; 547; and 555) and neighboring clergy and laity. He may ask: Should some parishes be merged? Should a priest be appointed the pastor of several neighboring parishes, as is permitted by canon 526, §1, such that he would be pastor of several neighboring parishes who would be served by auxiliary staff with him? Would it be more advantageous to appoint a "team ministry," envisioned in canon 517, §1?

It should also be mentioned that the provision of canon 517, §2 is seen as a kind of "temporary" measure due to a present shortage of available priests. Should that shortage cease, the ability to implement this provision would also cease. We may even say that the provision is "extraordinary" inasmuch as a pastor is viewed in law as proper to a parish by its very definition.

2. Is the "priest-moderator" the same as a pastor?

No. A study of the history of the development of canon 517, §2 shows that at times the canon was envisioned as saying he is the proper pastor of the parish. In the end, however, the promulgated law certainly does not make such a statement but says instead only that he is "endowed with the powers and faculties of a pastor." The *coetus* involved refrained from saying he is the proper pastor in order not to compress excessively the competence of those mentioned in the canon and to restrict excessively the role description of the new figure. The priest-moderator, then, is not the exact canonical equivalent of a pastor. Nonetheless, he is said to have the powers and faculties of a pastor (faculties, of course, are "powers to act.") This means he has the power to perform all the functions mentioned in the code as belonging to a pastor: e.g., the faculty to hear confessions within the jurisdiction of the parish (c. 968, §1); the faculty to assist at marriages within the confines of the parish (c. 1108, §1); the faculty to dispense from private vows under the conditions outlined in canon 1196, and so forth.

Inasmuch as he has the "power to act" as pastor, it is reasonable to assert that he is also the figure "who represents the parish in all juridic affairs in accord with the norm of law" (c. 532). He should "see to it that the goods of the parish are administered in accord with the norms of canons 1281-1288" (c. 532). Since he does all this, it follows that he should receive the counsel of the parish finance council as he administers parish goods (c. 537).

The code says the priest-moderator has the powers and faculties of a pastor. It carefully refrains from saying he also has all the pastor's obligations (e.g., the obligation to reside in a parish house close to the church, c. 533, §1).

The law also says that the priest-moderator has the powers and faculties of a pastor in the parish. In practice, the deacon or lay person may perform so many of the pastoral *munera* mentioned in canons 528 and 529. The priest-moderator must supervise that ministry. Also, if he is to perform that mission adequately it is reasonable to expect that he receive the counsel of the parish pastoral council whose president he is (c. 536). This council exists so that the Christian faithful "along with those who share in the pastoral care of the parish in virtue of their office give their help in fostering pastoral activity" (c. 536, §1).

Finally, since the priest-moderator is not the exact canonical equivalent of a pastor, it follows that he does not take canonical possession of the parish by formal installation (c. 527, §2); at least, the law does not specify that such must de done. Nor is he required to make the profession of faith at the beginning of his ministry (c. 833, 6°). He does not enjoy stability in office as does a pastor (c. 522). It is not appropriate to pursue the processes for his removal or transfer mentioned in canons 1740-1752.

3. What is the role of the parish coordinator?

The code does not specify in detail what particular roles should be given to the parish coordinator. This allows for creative possibilities to respond to the needs of the parish community in accord with the provisions of the law. The code simply says that the parish coordinator has "a participation in the exercise of the pastoral care of a parish." It is clear that he or she or they may be performing many of the pastoral roles mentioned in canons 528 and 529, as said already above. The litany of responsibilities in those canons is extensive and allows for much adaptation. All listings of responsibilities for the parish coordinator must recall that this character has a "participation" in the exercise of pastoral care in the parish. The law insists that "full" pastoral care is reserved to the priest in any parish. From this it follows that the principal responsibility of the parish coordinator is to work very closely with, and following the guidance of the priest-moderator who supervises the pastoral care given to the parish.

Pay close attention to the individuals mentioned in canon 517, §2. We may be speaking of (1) a deacon, (2) a lay person, or (3) a community of persons who are not priests. The deacon may perform a vast variety of liturgical and sacramental services; preaching the Word of God (c. 764), baptizing (c. 861, §1), distributing the Holy Eucharist (c. 910), celebrating Eucharistic benediction (c. 943), assisting at marriages if properly delegated by the local ordinary or the priest-moderator (c. 1108, §1), etc.

If the parish coordinator is a lay person, the diocesan bishop may judge it prudent and pastorally proper to designate that person to perform some liturgical and sacramental functions, in accord with the norm of the law. The bishop may, for example, designate these ministers to be extraordinary Eucharistic ministers in light of canon 230, §3. If indeed there is a shortage of clergy and since the Eucharist is "the center of the parish assembly" (c. 528, §2), the sacrament to which all the other sacraments and works of the apostolate are closely related and directed (c. 897), it may be appropriate for the lay pastoral coordinator to be so designated.

I do not believe, however, that this designation should be given for the celebration of baptism. Baptism is celebrated much more rarely than is the Holy Eucharist distributed to the faithful. I believe that since this is so, the ordinary minister of baptism should confer it.

The bishop may decide, moreover, to appoint some of the pastoral coordinators (deacon or lay) to serve as procurators/advocates for the diocesan tribunal (c. 1483) or even as auditors (c. 1428).

4. What is the "title" or designation of the parish coordinator?

Once again, the code does not specify what name should be given to the deacon, lay person, or community of persons who have been entrusted with a share in the exercise of the pastoral care of the parish.

Some have recommended and used the term "lay pastor." This is not appropriate from a canonical perspective. "Pastor" (perhaps better rendered as "parish priest"—*parochus*) is a technical term whose holder is to be in the order of presbyter, as we saw earlier (c. 521, §1). To create the term "lay pastor" is to create a contradiction: one cannot simultaneously be presbyter and lay. Although the parish coordinator may perform many pastoral services, he or she should not be called the "lay pastor." Besides, as already mentioned, the parish coordinator is not appointed to perform all pastoral functions but instead has been given "a participation in the exercise of the pastoral care of a parish."

Some suggest the parish coordinator be known as the "parish/pastoral administrator." This designation, though common in the United States, may also raise some canonical questions. Canon 1279, §1 refers to an administrator as "the individual who immediately governs the (juridic) person." Certainly, administrators of juridic persons need not be clergy (see c. 1279, §2 et al.). If the juridic person being considered is a parish (c. 515, §3), the law says that it is the pastor who is to represent it in all juridic affairs in accord with the norm of law (c. 532). The priest-moderator, with the "power to act" as a pastor is the figure representing the parish in juridic affairs and, hence, canonically administering the parish. Besides, we will remember that "parochial administrator" (c. 539) is a technical term referring to the priest who substitutes for the pastor of a parish on a temporary basis. These considerations indicate that the parish coordinator not be designated "administrator" of the priest-moderator. Also, and very importantly, the parish coordinator performs a rich variety of pastoral services not limited simply to the temporal administration of the parish.

Some may suggest that the parish coordinator be called the "parish minister." This designation does not raise the canonical questions which "lay pastors" and "parish/pastoral administrator" raise. It may be objected, though, that the term "minister" is overused and not a clear designation of the pastoral role of the character. Perhaps a better designation is "parish/pastoral coordinator," the term I have selected here. Personally, I prefer this term. I believe that particular churches may continue the search for an accurate and acceptable designation of this figure.

5. Some arrangements involve a so-called "sacramental priest." Is this envisioned by the law?

The law makes no mention of this arrangement. The sacramental priest comes to the parish to celebrate the sacramental and liturgical services reserved to a priest. I believe it is best that these services be celebrated by the priest-moderator. If some other priest regularly serves as the sacramental priest, one may ask why he is not in fact appointed the priest-moderator. It certainly does not seem good pastoral practice for liturgical and sacramental functions to be celebrated by a series of priests who have no real attachment to the parish. For the priest-moderator to celebrate them appears quite appropriate.

If, however, a diocesan bishop insists that the priest-moderator not be the sacramental priest, care must be taken to provide the sacramental priest with the necessary canonical powers and faculties to perform fruitful and effective ministry. This provision of faculties, however, leads again to the question: if the sacramental priest is to have so many powers and faculties of a pastor, why not appoint him the priest-moderator who by law has a pastor's powers and faculties?

I may mention here that I do not see canon 517, §2 calling for one diocesan-wide priest-moderator to be appointed for the several, perhaps scattered, parishes staffed by the parish coordinators. The priest-moderator in such a setting would appear more as a "vicar for parishes without a resident pastor" (or some similar term) than a priest-moderator.

I believe the priest-moderator should be appointed only to one parish or to neighboring parishes (see c. 526, §1, which says the same about the pastor). In order that he perform his role well, it is imperative that he collaborate closely with the parish coordinator and visit the parish frequently. While he presumably cannot be as present as a resident pastor, he should nonetheless be familiar to the parishioners. He is a significant part of the parish. Besides, if the priest-moderator is to moderate effectively the pastoral care of the parish, he must first know its pastoral needs. It would not provide effective ministry if he were appointed to too many parishes simultaneously, especially if they were not neighboring.

6. Who appoints the parish coordinator?

The code very clearly gives the answer to this question: the diocesan bishop is to appoint the parish coordinator. This certainly does not imply that he alone is involved in the process whereby the prospective parish coordinator is screened. The bishop may rely upon the advice of the diocesan personnel board/director/vicar and other consultants or consultative groups. Recall that the code directs the diocesan bishop, when appointing a pastor or the priests in a "team ministry," to make a judgment on the priest's suitability by listening to the vicar forane, by conducting the appropriate investigations, and, if it is warranted, by listening to certain presbyters and lay persons (c. 524; 542, 2°). The bishop is also invited if he judges it opportune, to hear the pastor(s) and the vicar forane when appointing a parochial vicar (c. 547). When appointing a parish coordinator, the bishop may likewise decide to listen to the insights of the local dean, the priest-moderator, and certain other presbyters and lay persons.

In any event, it is not the priest-moderator, the parish pastoral council, the personnel board/director/vicar, or any other person or group, who appoints the parish coordinator. Only the diocesan bishop makes the appointment.

Suggestions:

Canon 517, §2 raises a series of canonical questions which should be addressed and, in time, most certainly will be. The canon itself does not provide details on how it should be implemented, on the relation of the individuals to each other, on the precise roles each person has. The study of the history of the development of the canon, together with an awareness of other canons in the code, is able to provide some direction in the implementation.

In light of all that has already been said, and having studied how the canon is being implemented in a number of dioceses throughout the United States, I wish now to offer very respectfully some suggestions. Admittedly, my thoughts are subject to maturation and modification in light of new discoveries and insights. I welcome the suggestions of others.

Suggestion 1: Determine if the conditions of the diocese recommend the implementation of this canon.

Canon 517, §2 says that it may be implemented only when there is a shortage of priests. The final determination must be made by the diocesan bishop. It would be wise, of course, for him to rely on counsel from his principal consultative bodies, perhaps especially the diocesan pastoral council and the presbyteral council, in assessing the dearth of priests. The diocesan bishop must ask: Are there other ways to make up for this shortage? Can some parishes be merged or closed? Can liturgical and sacramental celebrations be reduced in number so that a priest may be available to more than a single parish?

Suggestion 2: Determine whether the diocese is implementing canon 517, §2 or not.

I believe it is very difficult for an accurate survey to establish in how many parishes the provisions of canon 517, §2 have actually been implemented. Some dioceses which claim to have implemented the canon have appointed a canonical pastor (c. 519) to several neighboring parishes in which a variety of other ministers serve (e.g., DRE's, pastoral associates, parish visitors, youth ministers, etc.). This is an arrangement with much merit. However, this is not the precise arrangement envisioned by canon 517, §2. In this canon the priest is not the canonical pastor but the "priest-moderator," as already mentioned.

In the final analysis, the services of the parish may be rather identical in either arrangement. The arrangements are not, however, canonically the same. From the outset, then, and for canonical accuracy, we must ask: Does the diocesan bishop wish to implement canon 517, §2? Or, would he rather appoint a canonical pastor to several neighboring parishes in which other pastoral "ministers" would serve with the parish priest?

Suggestion 3: Create diocesan guidelines for the implementation of canon 517, §2.

Several dioceses have implemented canon 517, §2, but very few have created guidelines for it. There is reason to urge the creation of guidelines to lead this implementation. In his pastoral letter on ministries, "In Service of One Another," Joseph Cardinal Bernardin said, "We shall find affirmation, coordination, and direction for ministry in the measure that we move toward clarification." Guidelines to lead the implementation of this canon would provide the basis precisely for such clarification.

Guidelines should address a number of issues, and should provide canonical accuracy for all involved in the arrangement envisioned by canon 517, §2. They would provide answers to such basic questions as:
—What is the precise role of the priest-moderator vis à vis the parish coordinator? What is his relation to the parish, its various activities and celebrations?
—What are the precise pastoral, administrative, sacramental, educational, and other responsibilities of the priest-moderator and the parish coordinator? (Recall that these may differ from parish to parish and whether the parish coordinator is a deacon, a lay person, or a community of persons. If a community of persons is entrusted with a participation in the exercise of the pastoral care of a parish, it seems appropriate that one of them be designated the "leader." That person may be called the "parish coordina-

tor" and the others called "pastoral associates.")

—If a priest other than the priest-moderator regularly celebrates those functions reserved to a priest, what are his rights and responsibilities? What faculties are provided for him? What is his relation to the priest-moderator and the parish coordinator?

—By what process is the parish prepared for the appointment of a priest--moderator and a parish coordinator, rather than a (resident) pastor?

—What are the qualifications necessary to be considered for the role of parish coordinator: academic, prior experience in ministry, personal gifts and talents, competence and skills, willingness to take part in ongoing formation, etc.? What provisions will be given to assure continued professional growth: e.g., taking part in various diocesan workshops and institutes, allowance for attending workshops/seminars/conferences, time and funds for days of retreat and recollection, etc.?

—Will a "contract" or "working agreement" be provided for the parish coordinator? If so, it may address such things as: residence, accountability, salary and benefits (see cc. 231, §2; 281, §3), term of appointment (probationary period, option for renewal, resignation, removal), relation to others on the parish staff (e.g., DRE, liturgy coordinator, etc.), evaluation, etc.

—Will some diocesan official or agency (e.g., the personnel board/director/vicar) be responsible for assisting those involved in this arrangement?

Suggestion 4: Provide adequate support for the parish coordinator.

In practice in many situations the parish coordinators will be performing pastoral services on a daily basis in the parish. Diocesan agencies should be sensitive to provide them with the information and materials necessary to give adequate pastoral leadership. Care must be taken to include them on diocesan mailing lists. It may be prudent to invite them to several diocesan gatherings or deanery meetings in order to keep them abreast on diocesan happenings. It may be good, as well, to encourage parish coordinators to meet together regularly; such times together could provide support, could allow for the sharing of many pastoral concerns, and could be an important occasion for diocesan contact with the group of pastoral coordinators.

It may also be a tremendous support for the parish coordinators to commence their pastoral service in a liturgical celebration in the parish. It is common for catechists in dioceses and in parishes to begin their ministry in the midst of such a celebration. If the parish coordinator is truly to serve the community, then that service may be formally recognized and celebrated by the community. A public prayerful celebration seems in order.

Further, whatever else is a valued support for other parochial ministers should also be provided insofar as possible for parish coordinators: e.g., a system of evaluation, opportunities for personal growth, access to diocesan agencies, support from the diocesan bishop, etc. Perhaps some diocesan agency should be given the particular responsibility of assuring or providing support and assistance to all the persons involved in this arrangement.

Many dedicated, talented, and generous deacons and lay persons have kindly offered their cooperation and assistance in parishes. Canon 517, §2 gives the basis for an innovative and interesting means whereby these persons may participate in parochial leadership. While continuing to pray for and to promote vocations to the priesthood, the Church must be grateful for the arrangement permitted by canon 517, §2.

JOHN A. RENKEN, J.C.D.
Springfield, Illinois

SUBSTITUTION OF PRIESTLESS SERVICES
FOR THE SUNDAY OBLIGATION[1]

An Opinion

The law of the Church on Sundays and holy days obligation is found in canons 1247 and 1248 of the Code of Canon Law.

Canon 1247: On Sundays and other holy days of obligation the faithful are bound to participate in the Mass; they are also to abstain from those labors and business concerns which impede the worship to be rendered to God, the joy which is proper to the Lord's Day, or the proper relaxation of mind and body.

Canon 1248, §1: The precept of participating in the Mass is satisfied by assistance at a Mass which is celebrated anywhere in a Catholic rite either on the holy day or on the evening of the preceding day.

The obligation to participate in the celebration of the Eucharist on Sundays and holy days is fulfilled by attendance at any Catholic Mass, whether of the Latin rite or an Eastern Catholic rite, on the Sunday or holy day itself or on the evening before. The obligation can be fulfilled at any Mass, including a ritual Mass such as a wedding Mass. An anticipated Mass should not begin before four o'clock in the afternoon.

Physical attendance at Mass, both the Liturgy of the Word and the Liturgy of the Eucharist, is the minimum form of participation. Optimally, all in attendance should participate fully, by their inner devotion and attentiveness, by their gestures, by their vocal participation in prayer and song, by their gift at the Offertory, and by their reception of Holy Communion.

At times it may be impossible to fulfill the Sunday obligation. Some examples include: when there is no Mass being celebrated in the area; when a person is prevented from getting to church due to illness, old age, or another reason; on a trip when someone through no fault of his or her own is unable to locate a Catholic church. Impossibility to observe the law is an excusing cause; there is no sin, venial or mortal, when it is impossible to attend Mass on a day of precept.

When it is impossible to fulfill the precept to attend Mass on a Sunday or holy day, canon law recommends the following alternative:

[1]From: *Roman Replies and CLSA Advisory Opinions* 1989, William A. Schumacher and Lynn Jarrell, eds. (Washington, D.C.: Canon Law Society of America, 1989) 95-96.

Canon 1248, §2: If because of a lack of an ordained minister or for other grave cause participation in the celebration of the Eucharist is impossible, it is specifically recommended that the faithful take part in the Liturgy of the Word if it is celebrated in the parish church or in another sacred place according to the prescriptions of the diocesan bishop, or engage in prayer for an appropriate amount of time personally or in a family or, as occasion offers, in groups of families.

The Church recognizes that in many areas of the world the faithful are not able to attend Mass every Sunday and holy day due to the shortage of priests. As a result, it recommends alternate ways for the Catholic people to keep holy the Lord's Day and the other holy days. When it is not possible to attend Mass on a day of precept, faithful Catholics can maintain the special character of these days by attending an alternate service at their parish church, or engaging in prayer personally, in families, and/or in groups.

These latter practices are not required by law; they are recommendations. One cannot say that they technically fulfill the legal obligation to attend Mass; rather, they are praiseworthy ways of observing the sacred character of Sundays and holy days when it is impossible for any reason to participate in the Eucharistic celebration.

JOHN M. HUELS, O.S.M., J.C.D.
Chicago, Illinois

PAROCHIAL STRUCTURES[1]

Parish Council

A parish council is a parochial structure consisting of representative members of the parish who form one body with the pastor in fulfilling the Church's ministry. This new and evolving concept in church law results from the conciliar emphasis on the expanding role of the laity. Conciliar texts stressing the collaboration of clergy and faithful in the evangelization and sanctification tasks of the Church provide the broad context within which the concept of parish councils can be best understood (see W. Rademacher, *The Practical Guide for Parish Councils*). Although parish councils are not specified in detail in the conciliar documents, *Apostolicam actuositatem* 26 promotes the idea of councils at the parochial level.

Theologically, the right and duty of the laity to participate in parish councils are rooted in the grace of baptism and confirmation. Born out of the need for co-responsible leadership, the parish council is the locus for the effective participation of clergy and laity in the total mission of the parish as called for in Vatican II.

According to Vatican II, one of the chief principles of the apostolate of the Church is that the laity should shoulder all the tasks that belong to their vocation in the Church and in the world. This does not by any means imply disrupting the community, but rather strengthening it. Representative spiritual leadership, efficiency in accomplishing pastoral goals, spiritual growth, and renewal, as well as the utilization of sound administrative procedures are some of the values that indicate a need for parish councils today. The parish council is considered to be a vital component of each parish.

Vatican II has affirmed that the diocesan bishop has ample freedom to structure parishes so as to provide the best possible service to the people in his care. Hence, after consulting his presbyteral council, he may require parish councils to be established in all parishes, and he may indicate the parameters of authority of such bodies.

The presence of both pastor and council members is necessary for the council to be effective. Because he is ultimately responsible for the care of the parish, the pastor presides at the parish council in a way strikingly similar to his presidency at the Eucharist. The pastor's ex officio role would not

---

[1]Précis of commentary, Janicki, Joseph A., "Chapter VI: Parishes, Pastors, and Parochial Vicars (cc. 515-552)" in *The Code of Canon Law: A Text and Commentary*, ed. James A. Coriden, et al. (New York/Mawhah: Paulist Press, 1985) 415-443.

preclude an elected member's conducting the regular meetings of the council; in fact, such an approach may be preferred. The presiding role of the pastor has to be seen within the context of the process of decision-making which involves many stages (see R. Kennedy, "Shared Responsibility in Ecclesial Decision-Making" in *Studia Canonica* 15 [1980]: 5-23). Kennedy distinguishes between decision-making (*a process*) and choice-making (*a part of the process*). He traces several stages of this process which include producing creative ideas, gathering factual data, making a choice among alternative options, implementing and evaluating the choice. Integral to each stage of the parish decision--making is the collaboration of the pastor and the parish council. In virtue of his office the pastor presides over and ratifies those stages of the process leading up to and including the final choice and its implementation. This role cannot be surrendered or diminished nor should authority be viewed as personal power, but rather as genuine service to the Christian faithful exercised in a collegial way.

For the sake of accountability to the diocesan bishop whom he represents and the people of God whom he serves, the pastor must ratify the recommendations of the parish council before they can be implemented. Likewise, the pastor must prevent the parish council from endorsing proposals which would be contrary to universal church law, diocesan statutes, or civil law.

Besides the pastor, others who share in the pastoral care of the parish in virtue of their office should be included: the associate pastor(s), deacons, lay ministers, director of religious education, teachers, and other hired personnel—some of whom may not actually be members of the parish. Not all of these need be ex officio members of the parish council. The forum provided by the council enables all to collaborate in fostering pastoral activity, i.e., an organized, unified endeavor, which broadly includes liturgy, education, social service, evangelization, mission activity, family life, communications, ecumenism, and administration. Parish council committees frequently respond to these areas of concern. The ministry of the parish council ought to be coextensive with the total mission of the parish. The parish council is a consultative body, that is one that provides advice in the process of decision making.

Finance Council

It is a new concept in the law that every parish must have a finance council. The parish finance council is a specific example of the general principle in canon 1280 that every juridic person must have a council or at least two consultors who will assist the administrator in fulfilling his or her responsibilities.

Unlike the law regulating diocesan finance councils (cc. 492-493), canon 537 does not specify the constitutive elements of the parish finance council other than by referring generically to universal law and episcopal norms. Therefore, since every legitimately established parish bears a juridic personality (c. 515, §3), the provisions of Book V of the Code of Canon Law, Title II ("Administration of Goods") apply. Other norms are relegated to particular law and need to be issued by the diocesan bishop to regulate uniformly the composition of the finance council and its duties. The diocesan bishop, for example, could determine the instances in which the administrator of a parish needs to consult the parish finance council for the validity of financial actions. The bishop also could set limits for financial actions which could not be exceeded on the parish level without his written permission. In some instances there could be some overlapping with the parish council and/or civil corporation structures of the parish, and it would seem advantageous for the diocesan norms to specify these relationships.

ADMITTING BAPTIZED CHRISTIANS TO FULL COMMUNION[1]

What jurisdiction is needed to receive a baptized Christian into full communion with the Catholic Church? For example, could the profession of faith be received by a lay person, such as a director of religious education, who would ask the local pastor to record it after the reception? Another example is this: if someone wishes to be received into the Catholic Church but does not wish to enter the RCIA process in the local parish, but instead prefers to receive private instructions from a friend involved in campus ministry at a nearby college, may this be done? Does it make a difference if the campus minister is a lay person or cleric? If the campus minister is able to receive the person into full communion with the Catholic Church, would the minister have the reception recorded in baptismal records of the person's proper parish, or of the parish in whose territory the profession of faith was made?

An Opinion

The query has two major issues: (1) who is the minister authorized to receive baptized Christians into full communion with the Catholic Church; (2) no matter who the authorized minister is, must a baptized Christian be received into full communion in their proper parish, or can this be done in some other place?

In answer to the first question, the norms governing the reception of baptized Christians into full communion with the Catholic Church are found in the 1988 revised version of the *Rite for Christian Initiation of Adults*. This has been normative for the Catholic Church in the United States since September 1, 1988. Specifically, Part II (Rites for Particular Circumstances), number 5 (Reception of Baptized Christians into the Full Communion of the Catholic Church), sets the norms which are to be observed.

Number 481 states: "It is the office of the bishop to receive baptized Christians into the full communion of the Catholic Church." Thus, as to what jurisdiction is needed to receive a baptized Christian into full communion, the answer is quite simply, the jurisdiction of the diocesan bishop.

But this does not mean the diocesan bishop must perform this rite personally for all such persons being received into full communion with the Catholic Church. The ritual continues, "a priest to whom the bishop entrusts the celebration of the rite has the faculty of confirming the candidate within

[1]From: *Roman Replies and CLSA Advisory Opinions* 1989, William A. Schumacher and Lynn Jarrell, eds. (Washington, D.C.: Canon Law Society of America, 1989) 87-90.

the rite of reception, unless the person received has already been validly confirmed." Thus, a priest may clearly be delegated by the bishop to receive a baptized Christian into full communion.

The ritual describes two ceremonies for receiving the profession of faith, one within the celebration of the Eucharist and the other outside such a celebration. In each case, the celebrant is clearly a priest (nos. 490; 502). Moreover, only a priest can receive the faculty, either from the law or by delegation from the bishop, to confirm, and confirmation normally is administered at the same time as the person is admitted to full communion as part of the full initiation of the person.

So in regard to the question, could the profession of faith be received by a lay person, the answer is generally no. However, it may be argued that under special circumstances a lay person could be authorized to receive a baptized Christian into full communion. The basis for this is canon 861, §2 concerning the minister of baptism: "If the ordinary minister is absent or impeded, a catechist or other person deputed for this function by the local ordinary confers baptism licitly." This is in addition to a "case of necessity" when "any person with the right intention" licitly confers baptism. If the bishop can depute a catechist or other lay person to administer baptism when the ordinary minister (bishop, priest, or deacon) is absent or impeded, by analogy it would be possible for the bishop to depute a catechist, director of religious education, or other lay person to receive the profession of faith and admit a baptized Christian into full communion with the Catholic Church.

The possibility would exist if the ordinary minister (bishop, or priest delegated by the bishop) were absent or impeded from carrying out this function. It could not be simply presumed by the lay person they are authorized to perform this rite, however, for the deputation of the bishop is needed, as it is for a priest to receive such a person into full communion. For priests this is often given in the diocesan faculties issued to each priest individually, which are habitual faculties (c. 132, §1). For catechists, directors of religious education, or the like, it could be granted in an habitual manner, as an habitual faculty, or it could be delegated for a specific case or cases. In either event, the lay person would not be able to confirm the newly received Catholic, although in a celebration of reception it would be possible for a properly authorized extraordinary minister of the Eucharist to administer Communion to the newly received Catholic.

The second question in the query relates to the place where reception into full communion takes place. It should first be clarified that a baptized Christian is not a catechumen, and should not be confused with one (see *Rite for Christian Initiation of Adults*, no. 477: "Anything that would equate candidates for reception with those who are catechumens is to be absolutely avoided."). While they are not permitted to be regarded as catechumens, they are "to receive both doctrinal and spiritual preparation, adapted to individual pastoral requirements" (no. 477). Instead of the liturgical rites of the catechumenate, they may benefit from the rites included in "Preparation of Uncatechized Adults for Confirmation and Eucharist" which are given in Part II, 4, of the *Rite for Christian Initiation of Adults* (see no. 478).

It would seem that baptized Christians are not restricted to their proper parish in becoming prepared for full communion in the Catholic Church. Neither the *Rite for Christian Initiation of Adults* nor the Code of Canon Law restricts this preparation to the person's proper parish.

Instruction prior to reception into full communion is not limited to clergy. Indeed, the *Rite for Christian Initiation of Adults* encourages that someone who has "had the principal part in guiding or preparing the candidates . . . should be the sponsor" at the rite of reception (no. 483). It is the competence of a person to prepare a candidate, rather than status as cleric or lay person, which determines who prepares the person for reception into full communion.

Whether the preparation has been done in or apart from the candidate's proper parish, the rite of reception does not seem limited to that parish. It pertains first to the diocesan bishop to perform the rite. He can designate another priest or, as argued above, under special circumstances another person, to receive the candidate into full communion. The bishop is not limited to parish boundaries in doing this. So it would be possible for a campus minister, properly delegated by the bishop in light of the above, to receive the candidate into full communion even outside a parish church.

The *Rite for Christian Initiation of Adults* calls for reception to be recorded "in a special book" (no. 486). Unless the bishops' conference specifies otherwise, this book would appear to be the baptismal register (c. 535, §1); so far as I know, the NCCB has not made any specifications in this regard. If confirmation has also been administered as part of reception, it is also to be noted (c. 895). Such registers are to be kept in parishes. If the campus ministry has been established as a parish (c. 813) it would have such a register of its own, and the event would be recorded there. If it is not erected as a parish, it would be recorded in the book of the parish in which the campus is located. The principle is that the event should be recorded in the book of the place where the rite took place, wherever that may be.

JAMES H. PROVOST, J.C.D.
Washington, D.C.

RECEPTION OF BAPTIZED NON-CATHOLICS
WHO ARE DIVORCED AND REMARRIED[1]

1. May baptized non-Catholics who have been divorced and remarried be permitted to be "welcomed in the catechumenate" when their marriage case has not yet been decided by the tribunal?

An Opinion

Irrespective of their marital status, baptized non-Catholics may never be "welcomed into the catechumenate" in the technical sense. The *Rite for the Christian Initiation of Adults*, no. 477, states quite explicitly: "Anything that would equate candidates for reception with those who are catechumens is to be absolutely avoided." The "National Statutes for the Catechumenate" of the NCCB emphasize: "Those who have already been baptized in another Church or ecclesial community should not be treated as catechumens or so designated" (30).

However, *RCIA*, no. 478, does permit the use of one or several of the special rites developed for the preparation of baptized but uncatechized (Catholic) adults for confirmation and Eucharist. Even here, the *RCIA* adds this note: "In all cases, however, discernment should be made regarding the length of catechetical formation required for each individual candidate for reception into the full communion of the Catholic Church." In other words, the process must be individualized, and not made into some prepackaged program.

Among the rites which can be used during the preparation of such baptized non-Catholics for reception into full communion is the "Rite of Welcoming the Candidates."

So far as I can find, there is nothing in the *RCIA* or in the "National Statutes for the Catechumenate" which prohibits welcoming divorced and remarried baptized non-Catholics as candidates for reception into full communion, even before their marital situation has received a definitive decision from the tribunal. In practice it has often proved beneficial to include as part of the conversion process a careful review of one's life such as is often conducted in the process of gathering evidence in a marriage case.

[1]From: *Roman Replies and CLSA Advisory Opinions* 1989, William A. Schumacher and Lynn Jarrell, eds. (Washington, D.C.: Canon Law Society of America, 1989) 86-87.

2. If a negative decision is given by the tribunal in the case involving a baptized non-Catholic entering into full communion with the Catholic Church, could the "internal forum solution" be utilized and, if so, on what grounds?

An Opinion

This is a very delicate question. It involves two distinct but closely related issues, that of the advisability of admitting persons to full communion in the Catholic Church who will be in an irregular situation insofar as their marital status is concerned, and the possibility of admitting to the Eucharist divorced and remarried persons whose present union is not recognized in the Church.

Let me begin by clarifying that the so-called "internal forum solution," if it is truly internal forum, is not a question for external forum policy. If it is appropriate matter for a policy, it is no longer in the internal forum but has become an external forum activity.

Baptized non-Catholics who enter into full communion with the Catholic Church would be in no different condition in these situations from Catholics who have received a negative decision from the tribunal. However, in preparing such non-Catholics for reception into full ecclesial communion, it would be important to explain to them the pastoral practice of the Church for Catholics in such a situation.

JAMES H. PROVOST, J.C.D.
Washington, D.C.

THE SACRAMENT OF PENANCE

The new law on the sacrament of penance is contained in canons 959-991 and corresponds to canons 870-936 of the 1917 Code. Some simplification has occurred in the new law; the basic changes regard the law on general absolution and universal jurisdiction for confessors.

Regarding the subject of the sacrament, there has been little change. Canon 988 adds the word "*gravia*" to the obligation to confess one's sins annually. This is not a change, but a clarification. The 1917 Code demanded that Catholics confess their sins annually. The theologians interpret this as an obligation to confess only grave sin; the new law actually spells this out. It should be noted here that in the terminology of the new law, sins are not divided into mortal and venial, but rather grave and venial sins.

The eight canons in the 1917 Code concerning reservation of sins have been omitted.

Canons 961-963 deal with general absolution. General absolution can be given in danger of death, or when there is grave necessity (for example, the number of penitents). In order to receive general absolution, one must be properly disposed and have the intention to confess grave sins individually in due time. This intention is required for valid reception of the sacrament. Finally, it is clearly stated that when a person has received absolution from grave sin by general absolution, he or she is obliged to approach individual confession when the occasion arises and should not again receive general absolution unless a just cause intervenes.

Canon 964 states that the episcopal conference can establish norms for the place of confession provided, however, that the confessional seat have a grill between the penitent and the confessor so that those who wish to use it may do so. The option of face-to-face confession remains.

The major change in the sacrament is the fact of universal jurisdiction (cc. 967-968). In summary, the pope, cardinals and bishops, by the law itself, have jurisdiction to hear confessions anywhere in the world. This faculty of bishops, it should be noted, can be restricted by local ordinaries. Moreover, presbyters who have territorial faculties by reason of office or commission, by reason of law, have those faculties extended to anywhere in the world. This would include other ordinaries, the canon penitentiaries, pastors and others who take the place of the pastor, superiors of religious institutes or clerical societies of apostolic life of pontifical rite (for their own subject and residents in their houses). Those who receive territorial faculties by commission include the following:

1. Priests can receive such faculties from their own ordinary where they are incardinated. These priests, by the very fact of receiving such

119

faculties, have by law, faculties extended throughout the world. If the faculties are revoked by their own ordinary, they also lose such universal faculties. If they are outside their own diocese of incardination, and the faculties are revoked by another bishop, this revocation only applies to that territory. These faculties are lost by excardination.

2. Priests may receive faculties by commission from the ordinary of the place where they have domicile. In such cases, the ordinary should inform the ordinary of incardination. These faculties are lost by losing the domicile. If the faculties are revoked, the ordinaries should inform the ordinary of incardination or the religious superior. Nevertheless, when such faculties are given, even by the ordinary of domicile, rather that by the ordinary of incardination, the faculties are immediately extended by law to the universal Church.

Under the new law, habitual faculties to hear confessions must be given in writing (c. 973). As in the 1917 Code, those who have habitual faculties, either by reason of office or by reason of commission, can delegate others to hear confessions, but only *per modum actus*. Canon 132 states that habitual faculties are ruled by the same norms as those for delegated power. Canon 137 states that those who have delegated faculties (and faculties to hear confession by commission would be delegated faculties) may further delegate, but only *per modum actus*. The canon also states that those who have ordinary power (and this would include faculties to hear confession by reason of office) can delegate both *per modum actus* and for all cases, unless the law provides otherwise. Canon 969 states that only the local ordinary can grant habitual faculties to a visiting priest to hear confessions. As an interesting corollary, it would seem that if the ordinary were to grant habitual faculties to a priest who is only visiting the diocese or has only a quasi-domicile in that diocese, then the extension of those faculties to the universal Church would not apply.

As a result of this new legislation on universal jurisdiction, the canon on faculties to hear confession on the high seas has been omitted. It should also be noted that the requirement of special faculties for hearing confessions of religious women is also dropped from the new code.

Finally, it is important to note that the new code retains the *Ecclesia supplet* law in canon 144.

The twenty-six canons on indulgences in the 1917 Code have been reduced to six, and canon 997 of the revised code refers all other legislation regarding the concession and use of indulgences to special law such as the *Enchiridion Indulgentiarum*.

BERTRAM F. GRIFFIN, J.C.D.
Portland, Oregon

THE SACRAMENT OF ANOINTING OF THE SICK

These canons, 998-1007, correspond to canons 937-947 of the 1917 Code of Canon Law. Little change has been made. The few changes that have been made can be reduced to four.

1. The title of the sacrament, as we know, has been changed from extreme unction to anointing of the sick. With this change, the title in law is also changed.

2. Now, oil may be blessed by any presbyter during the celebration of the sacrament and in case of necessity (c. 999). In the former law, a presbyter needed an indult from the Holy See.

3. Now, oil may be kept personally by every priest for cases of emergency (c. 1003, §3). Under the former law, pastors needed permission of the bishop to retain oils in their home or rectory.

4. The concept of conditional anointing is eliminated. In cases of doubt, regarding the use of reason, the degree of danger of the infirmity, or doubt regarding death, the law states now that the priest may anoint. Under the previous law they were advised to anoint conditionally (c. 1005).

The rest of the law is substantially the same. Only a presbyter or a bishop may administer the sacrament and the conditions for reception are the same as in the old law—that the persons to be anointed have reached the age of discretion or have the use of reason, that the person be a baptized member of the faithful, and that the person be dangerously or seriously ill, or in danger because of old age.

Besides the above mentioned changes, three collateral issues should be discussed.

1. Refusal of the Sacrament. The new law, canon 1007, is substantially the same as canon 942 of the 1917 Code. The word "mortal" sin has been changed to "grave" sin as occurs throughout the new law. Under the 1917 Code, manifest, grave and obstinate sin is a reason for the refusal of the sacrament of anointing. Moreover, the excommunicated (c. 1282) and the interdicted (c. 1283) were forbidden to receive this sacrament. There was some debate in the October, 1981 meeting about eliminating this restriction, but to no avail. Nevertheless, the new code does give wide discretion to confessors in remitting penalties, and hence, indirectly permits the administration of the anointing of the sick in all but the most cantankerous of people. Canon 976, for example, states that in danger of death, any priest can absolve from any sin or censure. Canon 1357 states that outside the danger of death, a confessor can remit *latae sententiae* excommunications and interdicts (which has not been declared or reserved to the Holy See) when a penitent finds it

difficult to remain in a state of grave sin for the time necessary to have recourse to a competent superior. Even when absolved, however, the penitent, either directly or through the confessor, must have recourse within a month. It should also be noted that this obligation to recur applies to those absolved in danger of death if they recover, and the censure was declared, imposed or reserved to the Holy See.

2. The second issue is that of *communicatio in sacris*. The whole discipline had been changed by the Second Vatican Council and is contained in canon 844.

The sacraments of penance, Eucharist and anointing of the sick can now be shared in the following circumstances.

Catholics can receive these sacraments from non-Catholic ministers under four conditions:

a. necessity or true spiritual utility;
b. no danger of error or indifferentism;
c. physical or moral impossibility of receiving the sacraments from a Catholic minister;
d. assurance that the sacraments in the non-Catholic church are valid (c. 844, §2).

The Orthodox may receive the sacraments of penance, Eucharist and anointing of the sick from Catholic ministers when they spontaneously ask for the sacraments and are rightly disposed. This privilege can be extended to members of other churches if the Holy See so judges (c. 844, §3).

Other baptized non-Catholics may also receive these sacraments under six conditions:

a. they cannot approach their own ministers;
b. they spontaneously request the sacrament;
c. they are rightly disposed;
d. they manifest Catholic faith regarding these sacraments;
e. they are in danger of death;
f. or if there is another grave necessity in the judgment of either the diocesan bishop or the episcopal conference (c. 844, §4).

General norms of the above cases can be given by the bishop or episcopal conference, but only after appropriate ecumenical consultation (c. 844, §5).

3. The final collateral issue is the pastoral theological issues which have emerged in this country, both from the ministry of permanent deacons who have sought permission to celebrate the sacrament of the anointing of the sick, and from parish experiences in common celebrations of the sacrament when parents bring infant children to be anointed. On the basis of these experiences, sometimes the question is posed even more theoretically: Is the sacrament of anointing an extension of baptismal healing, or is it specifically an extension of *Pax*, or sacrament of reconciliation, as was traditionally taught? Without

solving the theoretical debate, the present law retains the historical restrictions. Only presbyters and bishops can celebrate the sacrament, and in order to receive the sacrament, the person must have reached the age of discretion or have the use of reason. The usual reason given for these restrictions is that the sacrament, like the *Pax*, or reconciliation, grants forgiveness of sins and reconciliation with the Church, if necessary, and hence can only be celebrated by the bishop or his presbyters, who preside over reconciliation. Moreover, the person receiving the sacrament must be of an age when the sacrament of reconciliation could also be received. Other pastoral theologians have been maintaining that the sacrament is separable from the sacrament of reconciliation and can be viewed as an extension of the healing of baptism, that therefore deacons could celebrate the sacrament and, just as infants can be baptized, so they could benefit from this sacrament of healing. The theoretical discussion will still probably continue.

The new code does have a definition of the anointing of the sick which was not contained in the 1917 Code. Canon 998 states the Church commends the dangerously (or seriously) ill to the suffering and glorified Lord, that He may raise them up and save them. Though the theoretical issue is not resolved and would not be resolved by the law, the pastoral question has been resolved. Only priests can celebrate the sacrament (c. 1003, §1) and the recipient of the sacrament must have attained the use of reason (c. 1004, §1).

BERTRAM F. GRIFFIN, J.C.D.
Portland, Oregon

THE SACRAMENT OF ORDERS

The new law on the sacrament of orders is contained in canons 1008-1054 and corresponds to canons 948 through 1011 of the 1917 Code. Three major changes have occurred:

1. the definition of orders;
2. the introduction of the permanent diaconate;
3. the simplifying of the law on irregularities and impediments.

Canon 1009, §1 now defines orders as the episcopacy, presbyterate, and diaconate. The 1917 Code, which was modified by the Second Vatican Council, included under the concept of order or ordination, the consecration of bishops and first tonsure, as well as the major orders of presbyterate, diaconate, subdiaconate, and the four minor orders of porter, lector, exorcist and acolyte. Lector and acolyte are now no longer considered orders, but are lay ministries. Porter and exorcist or catechist are left to particular law and local initiatives. Subdiaconate has been dropped and is equivalent to the lay ministry of acolyte. First tonsure is replaced by the liturgical celebration of candidacy (c. 1034). Strictly speaking, however, one only becomes a cleric by ordination to the diaconate (c. 266, §1).

An interesting comment could be made regarding the shift in popular language. Although the language bishop, presbyter and deacon is contained in the 1917 Code of Canon Law, in popular language the sacrament was viewed as bishop, priest, and deacon. Since the Second Vatican Council, the use of the words "presbyter," "presbyterate," "presbyteral council" have become accepted as popular parlance. In canonical language, the word *sacerdos* includes both *episcopus* and *presbyter*. When the law says *presbyter* it means only that; when the law says *sacerdos* it means to include both bishop and presbyter. Hence, the accurate legal description of the sacrament of orders would be the division into priesthood and diaconate (or ordained ministry); and priesthood is divided into the fullness of priesthood or episcopacy, and the presbyteral order, which is a sharing in the ministerial priesthood of Christ and the episcopal order.

The section on requirements in ordinands and prerequisites for ordination has been somewhat simplified, obviously because of the whole reordering of the concept of orders. With the introduction of the permanent diaconate, the diaconal order is now divided into the transitional deacon (celibate), the celibate permanent deacon, and the married permanent deacon. Ages for the reception of diaconate and presbyterate have been slightly modified. Under the 1917 Code a deacon had to be twenty-two years of age; under the new law, a transitional deacon must be twenty-three years of age, a celibate permanent deacon must be twenty-five years of age, and a married permanent deacon, thirty-five years of age. In the 1917 Code the presbyter has to be twenty-four years old; in the new law, he must be twenty-five. However, the new law permits the ordinary to dispense one year from these age restrictions.

According to canon 1037, candidates for transitional diaconate or permanent celibate diaconate must make a public acceptance of celibacy prior to reception of the sacrament, unless they are already in perpetual vows in a religious institute. Before receiving diaconate, a candidate must have received the lay ministries of lector and acolyte and exercised them. There must be a six month interval between the reception of acolyte and diaconate. There must also be a six month interval between the order of diaconate and presbyterate for transitional deacons.

The whole concept of *titulus* is omitted in the new law. Hence, there is no longer any reference to ordination under the title of benefice or personal patrimony or pension, or the more usual titles (at least in this country) of service to the diocese or missions, or the religious titles of poverty, common table, or congregation. One is now simply ordained for the service of the particular church, personal prelature, institute of consecrated life or society endowed with the faculty to incardinate (c. 265).

Finally, the six day retreat prior to orders has been changed to a five day retreat (c. 1039).

Some of the material of the old law is repeated in a new section called "Documents and Scrutiny." The law, however, has been somewhat simplified. Testimonial letters, banns, and other means of coming to a decision regarding fitness for orders, are left to the discretion of the diocesan bishop or major superior. The rector of the seminary or formation house must testify to the orthodoxy, piety, good morals, and aptitude for exercising ministry on the part of candidates. It also must be clear that the candidate has appropriate physical and mental health. The exams or canonical scrutinies prior to orders in the old law have been replaced by a testimonial of completed studies, although, obviously, particular law could still require examination by pastoral boards.

Similarly, there has been little change in the section on the celebration of orders and the minister. Canon 1010 of the revised code simplifies the rules on the time of celebration. In effect, the sacrament of orders can be celebrated on Sundays, holy days of obligation, or for pastoral reasons, any day of the week. Canon 1011 states that ordinations should be celebrated in the cathedral, but can be celebrated in other church or oratories of the diocese for pastoral reasons. The institute of dimissorial letters has been somewhat simplified, but the law remains that one should be ordained by one's own proper bishop or have dimissorials. One's proper bishop, however, is now determined by domicile or intention to serve the local church; place of origin is no longer relevant in determining the proper bishop.

The thorny law on irregularities and impediments has been considerably simplified from the 1917 Code, but is still far from simple. There are no invalidating impediments to the sacrament of orders. The only condition for valid reception is that the candidate be a baptized male (c. 1024). Impediments are either perpetual (which means they cease only by dispensation) or temporary (which means they cease by dispensation or by cessation of matter). Perpetual impediments are called irregularities. The expression "impediment" is reserved for the simple or temporary impediments. Secondly, irregularities and impediments can prevent the licit reception of orders and the licit exercise of orders already received.

The division of irregularities into irregularity by defect and delict is retained; however, only one irregularity by defect is in the new law, namely the irregularity of insanity. It should be noted, however, that the irregularity of psychic defect rendering one incapable of ministry is now specifically added to the irregularity of insanity in the new law. As in the old law, if insanity or psychic defect emerges after ordination, it acts as a temporary or simple impediment to the exercise of orders, until after professional consultation, the ordinary judges that the person in question is now fit to exercise such orders.

All other irregularities by defect have been dropped from the new law: illegitimacy (bastardy), physical handicap, epilepsy, demonic possession, bigamy, infamy of law, and the irregularity against judges who have passed the death sentence or executioners who have carried out a capital sentence. Irregularity by delict is now limited to five categories:

1. apostasy, heresy or schism;
2. attempted marriage while bound by the diriment impediment of *ligamen*, orders, or public and perpetual vows of chastity, or marriage with a woman bound by *ligamen* or vows;
3. voluntary homicide and the procuring of or cooperation with a completed abortion;
4. self-mutilation and attempted suicide;
5. performing a ministry (act of orders) reserved to bishops or presbyters when not so ordained, or when prohibited by a declared or imposed penalty.

The irregularities by delict of voluntary reception of non-Catholic baptism and clerics exercising the forbidden professions of doctor or surgeon if a death follows have also been dropped from the new law.

Three simple impediments remain:

1. marriage (unless destined for the permanent diaconate);
2. having an office forbidden to clerics which demands civil accountability;
3. being a neophyte until judged mature by the ordinary.

The former simple impediments of being children of non-Catholic parents, slaves, still subject to military service, and infamy of fact have been dropped.

The bishop can dispense from the following irregularities against the reception of orders (all else are reserved to the Holy See):

1. Insanity and psychic disorders (assuming, of course, that the ordinary, after consulting with the professional, judges that the disorder is cured and would no longer render a candidate unfit for ministry);
2. apostasy, heresy and schism (not public);
3. attempted marriage against the diriment impediments of *ligamen*, orders, or vows, if the delict is not public (ordinarily, one would assume that the attempted marriage would have also terminated);
4. self-mutilation and attempted suicide, unless the facts had been brought to court;
5. a deacon or lay person attempting to exercise a ministry (act of orders) reserved to bishops or presbyters, unless the matter had been referred to ecclesiastical court.

The bishop can dispense from all simple impediments against the reception of orders except that of existing marriage.

The bishop can dispense from all irregularities and impediments against the exercise of orders except:

1. those brought to the judicial forum;
2. attempted marriage against the diriment impediments of *ligamen*, orders, or vows if the delict is public;
3. the delicts of voluntary homicide or performing or positive cooperation in a completed abortion, even if the act is not public.

BERTRAM F. GRIFFIN, J.C.D.
Portland, Oregon

127

PERMANENT DEACONS[1]

In November 1984, the National Conference of Catholic Bishops (NCCB) gave final approval to revised set of guidelines for the permanent diaconate in this country.[2] In conjunction with the 1983 Code of Canon Law, these guidelines and appropriate diocesan guidelines constitute the law regarding deacons in the United States.

1. Three-fold ministry

a. Ministry of love and justice. Deacons are doing all sorts of things to provide the Church's service to the needy. The code (c. 288) exempts them from some activities forbidden to other clergy, such as assuming public offices which entail participation in civil power (c. 285, §3), various business activities (cc. 285, §4; 286), and active roles in political parties and labor unions (c. 287, §2). On the other hand, it binds them to refrain completely from all things unbecoming to the clerical state and to avoid other things which are alien to the clerical state (c. 285, §§1 and 2). Neither the laws nor the NCCB guidelines are very explicit on what these forbidden activities might be. Given the emphasis in the guidelines on the deacon's role in the world, considerable flexibility seems called for in determining what is "unbecoming" or "alien" to *his* clerical state, as distinct from that of presbyters.

b. Ministry of Word of God. A study book put out by the Bishops' Committee on the Liturgy concerning deacons (*The Deacon: Minister of Word and Sacrament*) is a very handy compilation of what deacons can and cannot do liturgically.

c. Ministry of Liturgy. The NCCB guidelines list the liturgical activities open to deacons. They are careful not to list that the deacon could announce the "let's proclaim the mystery of faith" after the institution narrative, a practice which had developed in this country. This has been declared by the Congregation for Sacraments and Divine Worship to be the province of the priest alone, and does not pertain to the deacon.

The deacon is now listed as an ordinary minister of the sacrament of baptism, may be given general delegation for marriages, and may sub-delegate this according to the usual norms. The deacon also exercises other liturgical

[1]Précis of an article by James H. Provost entitled "Permanent Deacons in the 1983 Code" in CLSA *Proceedings* 46 (1984) 175-191.

[2]*Permanent Deacons in the United States: Guidelines on Their Formation and Ministry*, 1984 Revision. Available from the Office of Publishing and Promotion Services, United States Catholic Conference, 3211 Fourth Street, N.E., Washington, D.C. 20017, Publication No. 974-2.

roles. He is, however, still forbidden to administer the sacrament of the sick. The code has adopted the position that this sacrament is intimately connected with the sacrament of penance, and so has retained the Tridentine norm that only a priest may anoint sacramentally. The canon lists this as for validity, so it is a constitutive law from which the diocesan bishop cannot dispense (c. 86).

2. Particular Leadership Role

a. Parish. Deacons cannot be named pastor (c. 521, §1), nor be included in the group named to pastor one or several parishes *in solidum* (c. 517, §1). They can be entrusted with the pastoral care of a community without a resident priest however, even in conjunction with a resident pastor (c. 517, §2). The NCCB guidelines view this as abnormal, for the deacon is not a "substitute priest."

If such an arrangement is made, however, there should be a ministerial contract detailing the responsibilities of the deacon, his rights, and the relationship that is to exist between him and the priest who is to supervise his pastoral work.

b. Small Christian Communities. The NCCB guidelines identify this as a specifically diaconal possibility, working with small groups within a parish. The code really does not go into this form of leadership; it is an area for local experimentation and development.

c. Chaplains. The code appears to restrict chaplaincy to priests (c. 564). As presented in the canons, a chaplain is expected to provide the sacrament of penance. What does this do in regard to deacons who are serving as "chaplains" in some institutions? It would seem that the law has not taken this situation into account, but it could be handled in a way similar to the parish situations; the deacon is not a canonical "chaplain," but may provide chaplaincy services within his competence. Indeed, his responsibility to care for the sick, the poor, and others who frequently receive the Church's care in institutional settings would argue for diaconal ministry there.

3. Diocesan Diaconal Organization

The NCCB guidelines presume a structure will be established to address specifically diaconal concerns within a diocese, and that dioceses where the permanent diaconate has been restored will have a program.

Director of Diaconate. The guidelines make a distinction between the director of the diaconate, who oversees the selection and formation process, and a possible vicar for deacons who looks to post-ordination concerns of deacons.

4. Formation of Deacons

a. Selection of Candidates. Deacons are clerics. Candidates for the permanent diaconate are subject to the same irregularities and impediments as candidates for the presbyterate, with the sole exception of marriage (c. 1042, 1°). This has special application to divorced and remarried persons, for attempting even a civil marriage while impeded by an existing bond constitutes one of the irregularities (c. 1041, 3°).

One final item to note in regard to selection is the age factor. The NCCB guidelines state the U.S. bishops have determined that both celibate and married permanent deacons must be thirty-five when ordained, although the bishop can dispense up to one year.

   b.   Formation of Deacons. The code requires permanent deacons to receive three years of formation (c. 236). Candidates are not to be ordained until they have finished the time of formation (c. 1032, §3). The guidelines provide for a variety of approaches to these three years and leave it up to local dioceses, in keeping with their pastoral situations and resources, to structure a program in keeping with the general requirements of theological, pastoral, and spiritual formation.

5.   Married Deacons

The NCCB guidelines reflect the provision of the code in regard to married deacons, both in terms of the written agreement of their wives in order for candidates to be ordained and in terms of the prohibition of remarriage after ordination if a deacon is widowed.

6.   Ministry and Life After Ordination

   a.   Assignment. As with any cleric, a deacon is bound to obey his bishop, and to accept a *munus* entrusted to him by his ordinary (c. 274, §2). The NCCB guidelines propose some further specification on how this is to be done, something which does not currently exist for priests' appointments. There is to be a written document which "very clearly" spells out the expectations of the diocese, of the particular community in and for which the deacon serves, and of the deacon himself. The document is to be developed in consultation with all three—the bishop, the community, and the deacon himself. The assignment is to be regularly evaluated, reviewed, and even revised from time to time. The kind of personnel process described here does exist in practice in some dioceses, but may be a new experience for others.

This process, however, presumes a stability among permanent deacons which may not be true in practice. Those with secular employment can and in many cases are moved by their employer to new locations where they are unable to continue the ministry agreed to with the bishop; they may even be transferred by their employer to another diocese. To whom does the deacon owe primary allegiance, to the employer who provides support for him and his family, or to the bishop? This will have to be worked out in individual cases, but it does bring up the final question, payment to deacons for their ministry.

b. Remuneration. The new code also provides for remuneration of clergy, and specific attention is paid to permanent deacons. First, celibate permanent deacons are treated as any other clerics—when they dedicate themselves to ecclesiastical ministry, they deserve a remuneration consistent with their condition (c. 281, §1). They are also entitled to social assistance for illness, incapacity, and old age (c. 281, §2).

Next the canon turns to married deacons. They have added responsibilities of family to consider, so their remuneration will have to take this into account. If they dedicate themselves completely to ecclesiastical ministry, they deserve a just or decent family wage (c. 281, §3). If they have a civil (secular) profession, one which pays them independently of the Church, they are to care for their own and their family's needs from that income (c. 281, §3).

THE PASTORAL CARE OF MARRIAGE

Canon 1063 directs that pastors are obliged to see that the proper ecclesial community offers assistance in both proximate and remote preparation for marriage. Canon 1064 directs the ordinary to coordinate such assistance using the experience and expertise of the laity.

Strictly speaking, the impedient impediments to marriage are eliminated. However, in nine cases the ordinary's permission is required. Seven of these are found in canon 1071. Some of these so-called permissions might well be delegated in diocesan faculties to the local pastor.

1. The marriage of transients;
2. Marriages forbidden or not acknowledged by civil law (for example, marriages of undocumented aliens who feel frightened about applying for a civil license, or marriages of senior citizens who do not wish the marriage to be recorded by the State);
3. A marriage of someone who has natural obligations to a former spouse or children;
4. The marriage of a minor when parents are unaware or reasonably unwilling;
5. Marriage by proxy;
6. Marriage of someone who has been excommunicated or interdicted;
7. The marriage of notorious ex-Catholics;
8. Ecumenical or mixed marriages (c. 1124);
9. A past or present condition (c. 1102, §§2-3).

Although ecumenical or mixed marriages are now no longer forbidden, permission of the ordinary is required. The promise on the part of the Catholic to raise the children Catholic, if possible, is maintained not only for marriages with the impediment of disparity of cult, but with mixed marriages and with marriages of a Catholic and a notorious ex-Catholic.

There are twelve diriment impediments in the new code:

Canon 1083 — The impediment of age—14 for girls and 16 for boys; the episcopal conference can recommend a higher age for liceity;

Canon 1084 — Impotence;

Canon 1085 — Previous bond;

Canon 1086 — Disparity of cult;

Canon 1087 — Sacred orders (despite earlier proposals, this impediment has been retained even for married deacons who are widowed and wish to remarry);

Canon 1088 — Public vows in a religious institute;

Canon 1089 — Kidnap of a woman;

Canon 1090 — Murder of spouse;

Canon 1091 — Consanguinity in the direct line and to the fourth degree collateral line. (It should be noted that the Germanic method of computing relationships has been adopted by the new code. Under the Roman system and the 1917 Code, collateral degree of relationship is computed by counting the longest line *dempto stirpe*. Under the new law, fourth degree collateral line refers to first cousins, but may also include the relationship of uncle and grand niece.);

Canon 1092 — Affinity in the direct line;

Canon 1093 — Public decency, in the first degree of the direct line;

Canon 1094 — Adoption in the direct line and the second degree collateral line (adopted brother and sister).

The ordinary and the pastor have general authority to witness marriages within their territory (c. 1108). Both can give general delegation to priests and deacons to assist at marriages within their territory.

General delegation must be given in writing (c. 1111, §2).

Personal pastors, by reason of their office, are limited to performing marriages within their territory, where at least one of the parties is a member of their personal parish (c. 1110). Hence, if a personal parish were set up for a university, the pastor would not have authority, even validly, to marry a young couple, unless one of the persons were a student at the university or a member of the faculty or staff. In order to avoid such problems, it would seem wise for the ordinary to grant general delegation for the entire diocese to parish priests assigned to personal parishes. It might also be appropriate in many dioceses to extend the pastor's general delegation throughout the diocese by general delegation from the ordinary.

The marriage should be celebrated in the proper parish of either party, or even in a parish where one of the parties may have a months residence, or in the case of transients, in the parish where they are presently residing. Marriages need no longer be celebrated by preference in the parish of the bride. With the permission of the ordinary or the proper pastor, marriages can be celebrated elsewhere (c. 1115). But the reference to domicile or quasi-domicile does not necessarily imply that the territorial parish is given preference since personal parishes also are territorial, but limited to members of a particular language, rite, ethnic origin, etc. in a given territory.

Marriages ordinarily should take place in the parish church. The pastor can permit a marriage to take place in another church or oratory within his territory. Outdoor marriages require the permission of the ordinary. An interesting note is that marriages between a Catholic and a non-baptized person can be celebrated either in a church or any other appropriate place and no permission is required (c. 1118).

BERTRAM F. GRIFFIN, J.C.D.
Portland, Oregon

134

CONSECRATED LIFE[1]

There is often a confusion of terminology, with consecrated life and religious life being used interchangeably.

Consecrated life is defined in the code as follows (c. 573):

1) Life consecrated by the profession of the evangelical counsels is a stable from of living by which the faithful, following Christ more closely under the action of the Holy Spirit, are totally dedicated to God who is loved most of all, so that, having dedicated themselves to His honor, the upbuilding of the Church, and the salvation of the world by a new and special title, they strive for the perfection of charity in service to the Kingdom of God and, having become an outstanding sign in the Church, they may foretell the heavenly glory.

2) Christian faithful who profess the evangelical counsels of chastity, poverty, and obedience by vows or other sacred bonds according to the proper laws of institutes freely assume this form of living in institutes of consecrated life canonically erected by competent church authority and through the charity to which these counsels lead they are joined to the Church and its mystery in a special way.

The essential elements of consecrated life are the profession of the evangelical counsels and a stable form of life.

The code's definition of **religious life** is (c. 607):

1) Religious life, as a consecration of the whole person, manifests in the Church a wonderful marriage brought about by God, a sign of the future age. Thus religious bring to perfection their full gift as a sacrifice offered to God by which their whole existence becomes a continuous worship of God in love.

2) A religious institute is a society in which members, according to proper law, pronounce public vows either perpetual or temporary, which are to be renewed when they have lapsed, and live a life in common as brothers or sisters.

3) The public witness to be rendered by religious to Christ and to the Church entails a separation from the world proper to the character and purpose of each institute.

The essential elements of religious life are the public profession of the evangelical counsels by vow and common life lived in community.

---

[1]From: "Consecrated Life: New Forms and New Institutes," Joseph A. Galante in CLSA *Proceedings* 48 (1986) 118-125.

The code defines a **secular institute** as follows (c. 710):

1) A secular institute is an institute of consecrated life in which the Christian faithful living in the world strive for the perfection of charity and work for the sanctification of the world especially from within.

The essential elements of secular institutes are the profession of the evangelical counsels and a stable form of life lived in the world.

Similar to consecrated life are **hermits** (c. 603):

1) Besides institutes of consecrated life, the Church recognizes the eremitic or anchoritic life by which the Christian faithful devote their life to the praise of God and salvation of the world through a stricter separation from the world, the silence of solitude, and assiduous prayer and penance.

2) A hermit is recognized in the law as one dedicated to God in a consecrated life if he or she publicly professes the three evangelical counsels, confirmed by a vow or other sacred bond, in the hands of the diocesan bishop, and observes his or her own plan of life under his direction.

The order of **virgins** (c. 604):

1) Similar to these forms of consecrated life is the order of virgins, who, committed to the holy plan of following Christ more closely, are consecrated to God by the diocesan bishop according to the approved liturgical rite, are betrothed mystically to Christ, the Son of God, and are dedicated to the service of the Church.

2) In order to observe their commitment more faithfully and to perform by mutual support service to the Church which is in harmony with their state, these virgins can form themselves into associations.

The essential elements are a stable rule and acceptance by a diocesan bishop.

And, not included under consecrated life are **societies of apostolic life** (c. 731):

1) Comparable to institutes of consecrated life are societies of apostolic life whose members without religious vows pursue the particular apostolic purpose of the society, and leading a life as brothers or sisters in common according to a particular manner of life, strive for the perfection of charity through the observance of the constitutions.

2) Among these there are societies in which the members embrace the evangelical counsels by some bond defined in the constitutions.

The essential elements are life in common directed toward a common apostolic purpose. The evangelical counsels may be professed but this is not essential.

JOSEPH A. GALANTE, J.C.D.
Rome, Italy

CATHOLIC EDUCATION

Canons 793 through 821 on Catholic education in the code replace the 1917 Code's canons 1372 to 1383 on schools. The material is reordered and somewhat developed, based partially on the Declaration on Christian Education of the Second Vatican Council. The new canons are arranged with three preliminary canons, then a chapter on schools, a chapter on Catholic universities, and a chapter on ecclesiastical universities.

The first two canons repeat the traditional doctrine of the right of parents to educate their children, the right of parents to assistance in this from civil society, and the right of the Church to educate in virtue of its mission.

Canon 795 defines *education*, quoting from Vatican II's Declaration on Christian Education: "True education is directed toward the formation of the human person in view of his final end, and the good of that society to which he belongs . . . children and young people thus should be helped to develop harmoniously their physical, moral, and intellectual qualities. They should be trained to acquire gradually a more perfect sense of responsibility . . . and acquire the right use of liberty . . . and be prepared to take their part in the life of society." *Catholic education* is defined as education in accordance with the principles of Catholic doctrine (c. 803, §2) and *Catholic religious education*, whether done in schools or in the mass media, is subject to the authority of the Church (c. 804, §1).

Schools

The prohibition of canon 1374 of the 1917 Code against Catholic children being sent to non-Catholic, neutral, or mixed schools without the permission of the ordinary and in accordance with instructions from the Holy See has been removed. In its place, the freedom of parents to choose schools is recognized (c. 797). They should choose schools in which Catholic education is provided, or at least they should provide such Catholic education themselves outside of schools (c. 798).

Canon 803 defines a Catholic school as a school moderated by ecclesiastical authority or a public ecclesiastic juridic person. For a school to use the names "Catholic" in its title, it must be recognized as Catholic by ecclesiastical authority in writing. Catholic religious education, as distinguished from Catholic education, or education in general, is subject to ecclesiastical authority (c. 804 corresponding to c. 1381 of the 1917 Code). The episcopal conference should publish general norms on Catholic religious education. The bishop develops policies and has vigilance over such education. The diocesan bishop also has the right to visit Catholic schools in his territory and to publish general policy regarding such Catholic schools (c. 805).

Finally, the local ordinary has the right to name and approve teachers of religion and, if necessary, to remove or demand that they be removed (c. 806).

Catholic Universities and Ecclesiastical Universities

In the 1917 Code, Catholic universities are described in canons 1376; 1377; 1378; 1379, §2; and 1380. These canons have been considerably developed in the new law. In addition to the code, the apostolic constitution *Ex corde Ecclesiae* of 15 August 1990 (*AAS* 82 [1990] 1475-1509) on Catholic universities specifies and defines the role of Catholic universities and ecclesiastical faculties by providing additional norms and elaborating the norms found in the code.

The basic distinction between Catholic universities and ecclesiastical universities is not in the 1917 Code and is new with the revised one. A *Catholic university*, faculty or institute of higher studies is defined as a university dedicated to higher human culture and the full promotion of the human person, and is an exercise of the teaching office of the Church (c. 807).

In Catholic universities, a faculty or institute of theology, or at least a chair of theology should be erected and lectures in Catholic teaching should be held (c. 811). An *ecclesiastical university*, on the other hand, is a function of the Church's specific office of announcing revealed truth, and is a university or faculty in which sacred disciplines are investigated and scientifically taught to the students. The main canonical difference between Catholic universities and ecclesiastical universities is the degree of subjection to ecclesiastical authority.

The 1917 Code (c. 1376) states that the canonical constitution of Catholic universities or faculties is reserved to the Holy See and the Holy See must also approve their statutes. The new code states the right of the Church to erect and moderate universities, and the role of the episcopal conference in making sure that Catholic universities are aptly distributed in the territory (c. 809). In revising the law, it was recommended that a phrase about legitimate scientific autonomy be inserted into this canon. In Catholic universities the competent ecclesiastical authority erects the faculty of theology, as we stated above (c. 811), and it is the role of the episcopal conference and the diocesan bishop to have vigilance over the principles of Catholic doctrine in Catholic universities. No Catholic university can bear the name "Catholic" without the consent of the competent ecclesiastical authority (c. 808). The original schema demanded concession of the Apostolic See. It is the ecclesiastical university which, in accordance with the new law, needs erection by the Holy See, its statutes as well as the *"Ratio Studiorum"* must be approved by the Holy See (c. 816).

For Catholic universities, the competent ecclesiastical authority would presumably be, therefore, the episcopal conference and the diocesan bishops. It should be noted that in the new code, the statutes of the Catholic

138

universities should determine which authority is competent to hire professors and to remove them in accordance with procedures determined in the statutes. A reference in the earlier schema to the power of the episcopal conference and the diocesan bishop to demand that teachers be removed for reasons of violation of faith and morals was deleted during the revision (c. 810). It is only those professors who treat theological disciplines that must have a mandate of a competent ecclesiastical authority (c. 812). In revising the law, the expression "canonical mission" was changed to "mandate," and the requirement that subjects connected with theology also demanded such a mandate was removed.

Finally, the new code directs diocesan bishops to be responsible for the pastoral care of the students at a Catholic university, either through the erection of a parish, or at least through the assignment of priests to this work. Moreover, the diocesan bishop should provide, even in non-Catholic universities, a Catholic university center, which can provide aid, especially spiritual, to the young people attending that university (c. 813).

In summary, the competent ecclesiastical authority grants permission for the use of the name "Catholic" in the title of a Catholic university, has vigilance over the principles of Catholic doctrine, is directed to erect a faculty, institute, or chair of theology, and confers a mandate on professors who teach theological disciplines. The competent ecclesiastical authority is presumably the episcopal conference and the local bishop, not the Holy See. The ecclesiastical authority does not have power to hire and fire other professors or interfere in the scientific autonomy of disciplines other than theology, unless of course, the statutes of the university were to give such authority.

Matters are quite different with *ecclesiastical universities*. As mentioned above, ecclesiastical universities cannot be erected without the approval of the Holy See and such universities must have their statutes approved by the Holy See (c. 816). Several of the canons regarding Catholic universities also apply to ecclesiastical universities: statutes of the ecclesiastical university must define the competent authority for naming professors and for seeing to their removal in accordance with procedures defined by the statutes. The vigilance of the episcopal conference and the diocesan bishop over the principles of Catholic doctrine in universities applies to the ecclesiastical university as well as the Catholic university. Professors of theological disciplines require a mandate from the competent ecclesiastical authority in the ecclesiastical university and the diocesan bishop is asked to take responsibility for the pastoral care of the students.

Finally, canon 1377 of the 1917 Code regarding academic grades which have canonical effect is repeated in the new law. Such academic degrees cannot be conferred except by universities or faculties erected or approved by the Holy See. The following are some examples of academic degrees which have canonical effect.

Canon 253, states that professors of philosophy, theology and canon law in seminaries must have a doctorate or license in a university or faculty recognized by the Holy See. In the section of procedure, judicial vicars and adjutant judicial vicars (c. 1420, §4), tribunal judges (c. 1421), the promoter of justice and the defender of the bond (c. 1435), must all have a doctorate or license in canon law. Advocates must have a doctorate or be otherwise expert in canon law (c. 1483). Bishops, in order to be eligible for promotion to the order of bishop, must have a doctorate or license in scripture, theology, or canon law in an institute approved by the Holy See, or at least have equivalent expertise (c. 378, §1, 5°), and the vicars general and episcopal vicars must have a doctorate or license in theology or canon law or at least equivalent expertise (c. 478, §1). Canon 1378 of the 1917 Code permitting doctors to wear a ring and requesting ordinaries to give preference in conferring certain offices and benefices to those who have at least a license has been dropped.

BERTRAM F. GRIFFIN, J.C.D.
Portland, Oregon

ECCLESIASTICAL SANCTIONS

The entire maze of canonical penalties has been considerably simplified in the new law. The canonical censures now remaining are excommunication, interdict from the sacraments, and suspension. Such penalties as infamy and local interdict have been dropped.

Excommunication entails basically three effects. A person excommunicated cannot act as a liturgical minister, cannot celebrate or receive the sacraments or sacramentals, and cannot hold ecclesiastical offices or ministries (c. 1331). *Latae sententiae*, or automatic, penalties have wider significance. However, in the rare case that an excommunication is declared or imposed, either by ecclesiastical trial or administrative process, additional effects accrue: the person is to be removed or liturgical action should cease if he attempts to act as a liturgical minister. All acts of office are invalid. Persons who are excommunicated cannot enjoy ecclesiastical privileges or validly obtain a dignity or ecclesiastical office, and lose all stipends, salaries, and ecclesiastical pensions.

Personal interdict against liturgical participation (c. 1332) means that the person so interdicted cannot act as a liturgical minister or celebrate or receive sacraments or sacramentals. Obviously the main difference between interdict and excommunication is the issue of ecclesiastical office or ministry.

When interdict is declared or imposed by an ecclesiastical trial or administrative process, then such a person would be removed or the liturgical action cease if he attempted to act as a liturgical minister.

There are now only seven automatic or *latae sententiae* excommunications. Five of these are reserved to the Apostolic See: desecration of the Blessed Sacrament (c. 1367), laying violent hands on the pope (c. 1370, §1), absolving an accomplice (c. 1378, §1), a bishop consecrating another bishop without mandate (both are excommunicated—c. 1382), and direct violation of the seal of confession (c. 1388, §1). The two remaining automatic excommunications are for apostasy, heresy, or schism (c. 1364, §1), and for a completed abortion (c. 1398).

There are five automatic liturgical interdicts: laying violent hands on a bishop (c. 1370, §2); simulating the Eucharist (c. 1378, §2); attempting to give invalid absolution (c. 1378, §2); false denunciation of a confessor (c. 1390, §1); and a religious who is not a cleric attempting marriage (c. 1394, §2).

In danger of death, any priest can absolve from any censure. Ordinarily, a confessor needs special faculties even for absolving from undeclared and non-reserved censures.

If a cleric commits a delict subject to automatic excommunication, he is by the very nature of the penalty of excommunication, suspended. If he commits

141

one of the delicts punishable by automatic liturgical interdict, he is also thereby suspended.

In addition, there are two further automatic suspensions in the new law: attempted marriage (c. 1394, §1) and receiving orders from someone other than one's proper bishop without dimissorial letters (c. 1383). It should be noted that a bishop conferring such order is suspended for one year from conferring additional orders.

Suspension refers only to clerics and includes all or some acts of the power of orders, all or some acts of the power of jurisdiction or Church government, and the exercise of all or some rights or functions belonging to an office. A suspension does not affect the right to remain in the rectory if such right is attached to the office; it does not affect the right to a decent living and support from the Church; if the penalty is *latae sententiae* it does not affect the right to continue administrating an office.

All censures must be imposed by due process, either through an ecclesiastical trial or by an administrative process. Even if a censure is imposed by an administrative decree, a clear process must be used. The person must be informed of accusations and proofs and has the right to defend him or herself (c. 1720). Two assessors must be used to weigh the arguments and proofs. An administrative decree cannot impose a perpetual penalty (c. 1342, §2) nor can a judge in particular cases (c. 1349).

Finally, administrative acts, even impositions of penalties, can be referred to the hierarchical superior if there is question of the legitimacy of the penalty, the violation of procedural norms, or the penalty is imposed because of facts that are not true.

The section on expiatory penalties (cc. 1336-1338) only applies to clerics and religious, and includes dismissal from the clerical state for grave scandal or for grave crimes. Even if a cleric is required to spend some time in a house of prayer or a "guest house," this is ordinarily nor considered penal, but an attempt to rehabilitate someone from alcohol or chemical dependency.

In the section on penances and penal remedies (cc. 1339-1340) it is important to note that public penances can never be imposed for non-public transgressions.

BERTRAM F. GRIFFIN, J.C.D.
Portland, Oregon

WHY STUDY PENAL LAW?

1. That you may study it and receive reward.

In the *Torah* we read: "If a man has a stubborn and rebellious son . . . his father and mother shall take hold of him and bring him out to the elders of his town . . . they shall say to the elders 'this son of ours is stubborn and rebellious . . . he is a glutton and a drunkard.' Thereupon the men of his town shall stone him to death" (*Deut* 21:18-21). In the *Talmud* the sages list all the restrictions against applying this penalty: Son means only a son not a daughter; son excludes children and adults and is limited to a boy at puberty only. He must be a glutton and a drunkard. If he drinks too much but is not a glutton, he is exempt. Both his father and his mother must seek his execution; if one demurs he is exempt. If his parents are lame, dumb, blind, and/or deaf then they cannot have a rebellious son—and on and on and on. Finally R. Judah comments, "there never has been a stubborn and rebellious son and never will be." R. Simeon adds, "because someone eats a pound of meat and drinks two cups of Italian wine, shall his father and mother have him stoned? It never happened and never will happen." Both ask, "why then was this law written?" And both answer, "that you may study it and receive reward" (*Sanhedrin* 71a).

The Code of Canon Law has an entire book (Book VI) on sanctionable offenses and penalties. Book VII contains a special section on penal procedures. Yet all canonists know how rarely penalties are declared or inflicted by the Church. The procedures are lengthy and cumbersome; the reasons excusing from imputability are many; the majority of the offenses defined in the code rarely occur. Why then was this law written? The study of penal law is basically a study of the limits of *communio*. The Church denies or restricts table fellowship and pastoral ministry for only the most serious of reasons, listed in canons 1364-1399. These canons reflect the legislator's concern to protect church unity and prevent or repair serious scandal and damage in church life. Penal law is not a code of moral and ethical behavior. Rather, it describes the limits which the Church requires of all members of the Catholic family for the sake of public order and the common good. The study of penal law reminds the student of those duties and obligations which the Church as an external, visible, and independent society considers minimal for the survival of church communion.

2. That the church authorities may learn compassion.

"The stubborn and rebellious son" is only one of twenty eight crimes listed in the *Torah* as punishable by death. The *Talmud* contains an exhaustive analysis of each of these crimes as well as the procedures of investigation, trial, and execution. Finally, after pages and pages of exegesis the *Mishna* states: "A Sanhedrin that effects an execution once in seven years is branded a destructive tribunal." R. Eliezer b. Azariah, a second generation rabbinical teacher after the destruction of the Temple and the cessation of capital punishment by rabbinic authority adds "once in seventy years." R. Tarfon and R. Akiva, third generation rabbinic teachers say, "had we been members of a Sanhedrin, no person would ever be put to death because of the rigorous proof we would demand" (*Makkoth* 7a).

The study of penal law not only defines the public limits of *communio*; it also defines the limits of coercive power and reminds church authority of the priority of pastoral care over punishment.

Canon 1341 permits the ordinary to impose or declare penalties only after three conditions have been met:

1. It is clear the scandal cannot be sufficiently repaired.
2. It is clear the justice cannot sufficiently be restored.
3. It is clear that the accused cannot sufficiently be reformed by other means such as: fraternal correction, rebuke, or pastoral care.

Moreover, this requirement must be met during the investigation prior to initiating either administrative or judicial proceedings (c. 1717, §1, 2°).

During the course of a trial or administrative procedure, in cases where the law demands a certain penalty, the judge or ordinary may still refrain from imposing the penalty or impose a lighter one if the accused has reformed and scandal has already been repaired. Punishment of the accused by civil authority is an additional reason for church authorities not to impose the prescribed penalty (c. 1344, §2).

When I was in the seminary (30 years ago) the class on pastoral practices was taught by a stern Sulpician who was also rector of the seminary and unbending in his interpretation of the seminary rule. During a lecture on denial of absolution in the confessional he warned us that we might have to deny absolution once in our priestly career. If we did it twice, he said we were bad confessors! My reading of penal law leads me to believe that an ordinary or judge should be equally compassionate and pastoral when it comes to declaring or inflicting ecclesiastical sanctions. Penal law, like the denial of absolution, is a last resort.

3. That church members may protect themselves against abuse of authority.

The Christian faithful have a fundamental right not to be punished with canonical penalties except in accord with the norm of law (c. 221, §3). Knowledge is power. There was a time when canon law was only in Latin. Now an English translation of the code including penal law is on every coffee table along with the "Fireside Edition" of the Bible. When everyone knows how ordinaries and judges are expected to behave, when abuse of authority is immediately exposed and challenged in the public media, every member of the Church is that much safer from arbitrary and whimsical imposition of sanctions.

BERTRAM F. GRIFFIN, J.C.D.
Portland, Oregon